Surviving
Personal
Bankruptcy

SURVIVING PERSONAL BANKRUPTCY

YOUR GUIDE TO THE PERSONAL, LEGAL, AND FINANCIAL ISSUES

NORA RAUM

GOTHAM BOOKS

GOTHAM BOOKS
Published by Penguin Group (USA) Inc.
375 Hudson Street, New York, New York 10014, U.S.A.

Penguin Group (Canada), 90 Eglinton Avenue East, Suite 700, Toronto, Ontario,
Canada M4P 243 (a division of Pearson Penguin Canada Inc.); Penguin Books Ltd,
80 Strand, London WC2R 0RL, England; Penguin Ireland, 25 St Stephen's Green,
Dublin 2, Ireland (a division of Penguin Books Ltd); Penguin Group (Australia),
250 Camberwell Road, Camberwell, Victoria 3124, Australia (a division of Pearson
Australia Group Pty Ltd); Penguin Books India Pvt Ltd, 11 Community Centre,
Panchsheel Park, New Delhi – 110 017, India; Penguin Group (NZ), cnr Airborne and
Rosedale Roads, Albany, Auckland 1310, New Zealand (a division of Pearson New
Zealand Ltd); Penguin Books (South Africa) (Pty) Ltd, 24 Sturdee Avenue, Rosebank,
Johannesburg 2196, South Africa

Penguin Books Ltd, Registered Offices: 80 Strand, London WC2R 0RL, England

Published by Gotham Books, a division of Penguin Group (USA) Inc.

First printing, April 2005
10 9 8 7 6 5 4 3 2 1

Copyright © 2005 by Nora Raum
All rights reserved

Gotham Books and the skyscraper logo are trademarks of Penguin Group (USA) Inc.

Library of Congress Cataloging-in-Publication Data
Raum, Nora.
   Surviving personal bankruptcy : your guide to the personal, legal, and financial issues
/ by Nora Raum.
      p.   cm.
   ISBN 1-59240-158-9 (alk. paper)
   1. Bankruptcy—United States—Popular works. 2. Finance, Personal—United
States—Popular works. I. Title.
   KF1524.6.R38 2005
   346.7307'8—dc22   2005001927

Printed in the United States of America

Set in Adobe Garamond and Escorial
Designed by Judith Stagnitto Abbate/Abbate Design

TO TOM

CONTENTS

Introduction   1

PART ONE: SAYING THE "B" WORD   3

Chapter One: Ten Signs That You Need This Book   5
Chapter Two: What Is Bankruptcy?   12
Chapter Three: Taking an Honest Look at Your Situation   17
Chapter Four: Frequently Asked Questions About Bankruptcy   22

PART TWO: WEIGHING YOUR OPTIONS   31

Chapter Five: "Chapter 7"—The Liquidation Bankruptcy   33
Chapter Six: "Chapter 13"—The "Wage-Earner's" Plan   38
Chapter Seven: Deciding Between Chapter 7 and Chapter 13   43
Chapter Eight: The 2005 Law   47
Chapter Nine: Alternatives to Bankruptcy   53

PART THREE: GETTING READY—
PREPARATION IS THE KEY   63

Chapter Ten: You Don't Have to Hire a Lawyer . . . but You Probably
Should   65

Chapter Eleven: Ten Tips for Selecting an Attorney   69
Chapter Twelve: Assembling the Paperwork   76
Chapter Thirteen: Pre-bankruptcy Do's and Don'ts   83

PART FOUR: THE PROCESS   91

Chapter Fourteen: The Filing   93
Chapter Fifteen: The Hearing   96
Chapter Sixteen: Tying Up the Loose Ends   101
Chapter Seventeen: Confronting the Things That Can Go Wrong   110

PART FIVE: LIFE AFTER BANKRUPTCY   119

Chapter Eighteen: Cleaning Up Your Credit Report   121
Chapter Nineteen: Establishing New Credit   126
Chapter Twenty: Look Out for the Scams   131

PART SIX: APPENDICES   135

Appendix I: Worksheets for Assessing Your Assets, Debts, and Budget   135
Appendix II: Tables of State-by-State Homestead Exemptions   141
Appendix III: State-by-State Median Income for a Family of Four (Sample)   143
Appendix IV: Worksheets for Assembling Information You Need for Filing   145
Appendix V: Sample Bankruptcy Petition   155
Appendix VI: Sample Letters to Creditors and Credit-Reporting Agencies   195

Bibliography   199
Acknowledgments   201
About the Author   203
Index   205

SURVIVING PERSONAL BANKRUPTCY

OKAY, so you're considering the "B" word. This book is designed to help you understand how bankruptcy works and whether it might be a good option for you. Bankruptcy is not the end of the road. It's merely a stop along the road to a better financial life.

The first thing you have to understand is that this is a business decision, not a moral one. Nobody will stamp a scarlet "B" on your forehead. Bankruptcy may not be the right way to go but you need to explore all your options. If you are considering bankruptcy enough to pick up this book, then you are probably in serious financial trouble. You have a whole bunch of lousy choices here and bankruptcy may well be the least lousy of them.

You should also understand that many, many people have been through this process. In fact, I open most chapters with a little story about someone famous who filed bankruptcy. People from all walks of life have chosen bankruptcy as a way to get out from under unmanageable debt.

Some people end up in bankruptcy court because they first made a stop in divorce court. A divorce can leave both parties in far worse financial shape. And if one person files bankruptcy, the other one may be forced to follow.

Another major reason for bankruptcy is the high cost of medical care. If you don't have insurance and you encounter any major health problem, you have no choice but to run up huge medical bills.

Many people find themselves in over their heads after chasing the American dream. They get tired of the uncertainties of the labor market and decide to strike out on their own and start their own businesses. Many small businesses fail and take their owners down with them.

I've seen it many times. A person sets up shop and puts everything into the business, and I do mean everything. She'll cash out her 401(k) from her last job and take out a second mortgage on her house. She'll use her own credit cards to keep the business going. Unless the business takes off—and most don't—she'll end up with no business, no job, a whole lot of debt, and nothing to show for it.

People end up filing bankruptcy for many different and legitimate reasons. So stop beating yourself up about how you got into this mess and start figuring out what you should do to get out of it.

This book is *not* designed to tell you everything you need to know to file your own bankruptcy without hiring an attorney. You may choose to do that, but if you do, you'll need to read many more books than this one.

Information is the key no matter what you decide to do. I'll explain what bankruptcy is and how it works. I'll give you some suggestions on how to analyze your situation to determine if bankruptcy may be right for you. I provide some easy-to-use worksheets and step-by-step instructions on how to get started. Sometimes the hardest part of any important job is to get going. This book will also discuss possible alternatives to bankruptcy.

Bankruptcy is a mystery to most people. They hear the word now and then, usually in connection with some huge corporation. But they have no idea what it means to people like them. They need basic information to help them decide if bankruptcy might be right for them.

After making that decision, they want to know what's involved. What happens at the hearing? Will my bank close my checking account? Will my landlord know? This book is designed to answer the basic questions and maybe some you hadn't thought of.

Finally, this book will explain what happens after the bankruptcy. I can't stress enough that bankruptcy is not the end of a process but just one step in improving your financial situation.

So how do I know all this? I've been a bankruptcy lawyer for nineteen years. I've seen for myself the positive effect it can have on people's lives. I watch the relief on my clients' faces at our first meeting when I explain their situation is not hopeless and I can help. I think that's what attracted me to this kind of law practice. I can make a real difference in people's lives.

Keep reading and let me help you make a difference in yours.

PART ONE

SAYING THE "B" WORD

CHAPTER ONE

TEN SIGNS THAT YOU NEED THIS BOOK

ALTHOUGH you picked up this book, you may still be denying to yourself that bankruptcy is a possibility. You may be right. But if some of the following signs are familiar, you might want to keep reading.

1. You're not sure how much you owe.

Ignorance is not bliss. It's a bad sign if you don't know how much you owe. I don't mean down to the exact penny, but a pretty good idea of your total indebtedness. People who are in serious financial trouble often will have no idea of the extent of their problem. I see this all the time. A client will tell me in the initial interview that she has around $20,000 in credit card bills. But when everything is added up, that figure will sometimes be close to twice that amount.

Part of this is simple denial. People don't really want to know how dire their situation is. So they just take a quick glance at the minimum payment due and let it go at that. That's if they open the bill at all. I've had clients bring me a bagful of unopened bills, some several months old.

Sometimes with married couples, one half leaves all the bill paying to the other and truly does not know what's going on. Occasionally, the rude awakening happens in my office. The wife will say, "We probably have about $30,000 in credit card debt."

The husband will turn in horror and say, "What!?" Then it will turn out they really owe $40,000.

Often, credit card companies will raise interest rates for the people least able to pay back the debt, without notifying the customers. The climbing balances will then push the debtor above his or her credit limit, which allows the creditor to impose over-limit fees as well. And don't forget the late fees. People who have been in denial over the extent of their indebtedness are truly shocked when they see what happened to their accounts while they weren't opening the bills.

Another factor is that some people have so many accounts that it is hard to keep track of it all. Which leads me to . . .

2. You have too much plastic.

Nobody needs three credit cards from Capital One. If you have more than two or three major credit cards, you are looking for trouble. People who are starting to drown in debt will sometimes grab another credit card as a life preserver. They get the "you are approved" letter in the mail and quickly send it back, hoping that a new source of credit will help them get out of their mess. But it just gets worse.

Some people do balance transfers as a way of life. They get an offer for a new card at a great "introductory" rate if they transfer the balance of another credit card. Although it sounds like a good idea—trading a high interest rate for a lower one—it doesn't always work that way.

Often, the introductory rate doesn't last long and the new interest rate could be even higher than the old one. Sometimes, people continue to use the old card rather than close it out. They run up more debt and wind up in even worse shape.

A client told me to make sure I include "payday" loans in my ten warning signs. The idea of such loans is to give the customer some cash until the next payday. The customer provides the lender with a postdated check or an authorization for the lender to withdraw money from a bank account. The customer gets the money today and pays back the full amount plus a fee. Sometimes, the lender will allow the balance to be paid in installments, but there is a hefty fee or interest rate.

These loans are ridiculously easy to get. They're even available over the Internet. They're easy to obtain because they're designed for desperate people. As my client says, once you start taking out payday loans, you know you're in trouble.

She speaks from experience.

3. You pay for food and other basic needs with credit cards.

Credit cards can be a useful tool in managing your finances, but you probably shouldn't be whipping out a card every time you go through the grocery checkout line. If you find yourself paying for the usual, basic expenses with plastic, you may be in more trouble than you think. It's very easy to find yourself running up huge debts with nothing to show for it.

Paying with a credit card can seem like not spending money at all. So you may buy stuff you might not buy if you had to spend cold, hard cash. When a credit card bill comes in, do you ever say, "What was I thinking?" You might not even be able to remember what you bought with the $27 you spent at the drugstore.

People in financial trouble can also develop a "what the heck?" attitude. They know their credit card balances are totally out of sight. They figure their situation is so hopeless that one more small purchase won't make much difference. This defeatist approach might be a warning sign by itself.

Routinely paying by credit card could also mean you never have any cash. What money you do have in the checking account is now going toward debt service—toward making those minimum payments every month. Beware if you find yourself using plastic to make very small purchases.

4. You rob Peter to pay Paul.

The credit card version of this is to use cash advances from one creditor to pay minimum payments on the others. Once you go down that path, you most likely won't be able to turn back. And that path could end up in bankruptcy court. Similarly, you may find yourself relying on your bank account's overdraft protection or a home equity line of credit just to keep going.

It's like your personal Ponzi scheme, where a constant infusion of new debt is needed just to keep up with the old debt. Eventually, the system will collapse of its own weight.

You never catch up this way. You simply add to your overall indebtedness. And if you do end up filing bankruptcy, creditors might point to this behavior as proof that you never intended to repay the debts since you were already broke when you incurred them.

I admit the credit card companies and banks make it all too easy. They'll send you checks even if you didn't ask for them. All you have to do is fill one out and sign it. It's as good as cash. Actually it's not as good as cash. It's really an I.O.U. that you can't afford to pay back.

The credit card companies also helpfully provide you with a personal identification number so that you can get cash out of the ATM. It's so tempting. You're out of money. You're out of milk. And the VISA payment is due. So you write a check on the Discover card to pay the minimum on the VISA. You stick the VISA card in the ATM to buy the milk. This solves your immediate problems but makes your long-term problems far worse.

5. Your credit cards are maxed out and you pay only the minimum.

You know you're in trouble when most of your cards are maxed out. You've hit your credit limit and can't charge any more. But all you can afford to pay is the minimum amount required. You can pay that minimum for the rest of your life and you'll never pay off the debt. Just take a look at how much of that payment goes to the principal. It's a small percentage. And the moment you're a day late, the credit card company will charge a late fee, charge an over-limit fee, and maybe jack up your interest rate as well. Yes, they can do that.

By the way, creditors love it when customers charge up to the maximum and then pay the minimum. That's how they make their money. Sometimes, they raise the credit limit to allow the customer to fall even further into debt.

Former clients often refer their friends to me. So I sometimes get a whole bunch of the same kind of client. For example, for a while I had a lot of Asian clients who worked in restaurants. Every one of them—Chinese cooks, Thai waiters—had a credit card with MBNA, with an outrageous credit limit.

They had charged up to the limit, while faithfully making the minimum payment every month. When they hit the limit, MBNA would raise it and they'd charge up to that. Some of them had credit limits of $15,000! In some cases, these guys were making less than the minimum wage. There is no reason why MBNA should have given them such high limits.

You have to wonder if that's what MBNA had in mind. My clients had been paying, literally for years, before they realized they'd never be able to pay it off. I think they each had paid off the actual balance, not counting the interest, several times over.

If it looks like I'm picking on MBNA, you may be right. It has an aggressive marketing department. It sets up tables at baseball parks, offering a "free" gift if fans sign up for a card with their team's logo.

I don't know if MBNA is more guilty of this than others. I just observed this "Asian food worker pattern" in my own practice. I know there are a lot of pushy credit card companies out there. This is just one example.

It's become almost stereotypical for clients to tell me that their credit card spending began in college. They'd get a "free" T-shirt if they signed up for the card. These were kids with no jobs and often little sense. They'd graduate from college with a $6,000 credit card bill and no recollection of how they spent it. Pizza, maybe?

They had charged up that card to the maximum and paid the minimum. So that led to another card and another card. They never did catch up and ended up in my office, embarrassed, some years later.

6. You rely on overtime to pay your basic expenses.

If you depend on overtime pay just to make basic expenses, you're going to hit the wall someday. Overtime may not be something you can count on where you work. Similarly, it's not a good sign if you depend on a second job to keep your head above water. It shows you're working too close to the edge. One small setback and it's all over.

You might be able to work all those hours for a while, but at some point the extra work could take its toll on you and your family. It will do no one any good if you run yourself into the ground.

Having to work extra might be another sign that too much money is going toward servicing your debt. If your basic pay used to be enough to pay your bills, and it isn't any longer, then you've probably increased your bills.

7. You kite checks.

You send off the minimum payment for the VISA bill and hope it's not presented to the bank for payment before your paycheck gets there. It's called "check kiting" and it's not only illegal in many jurisdictions, but it's a really bad idea.

Some pushy creditors will convince you to give them a postdated check or the authorization to deduct a payment from your checking account. They'll even tell you to pick a date in the not-too-distant future when the payment should be processed. This can be dangerous. First, the creditor might go ahead and process the payment before the agreed date. I know you won't be shocked when I tell you that bill collectors don't always keep their word.

Second, much could happen between now and then to keep you from having enough money in your account. If you suddenly need to rush your child to the emergency medical clinic, you're going to write a check to cover the expense, even if the money had been promised to Household Finance. There could be a mix-up with your job and your paycheck could be smaller than expected.

But mainly, check kiting is a sign that your finances are a mess. You shouldn't have to cut it so close.

8. You hide the evidence.

Maybe it's that denial thing again, but many people try to hide the extent of their debt from their loved ones, such as a parent or a spouse. If you're rushing to pick up the mail before your wife can get to it, you already know you're in trouble. You're just trying to keep from getting in trouble with her.

I don't mean to sound flippant here. Financial troubles can affect every part of one's life. I've noticed for years that bankruptcy and divorce can go together. Sometimes the pressures of overwhelming debt will cause a couple to break up. Or it can work the other way. A couple divorces and their financial problems double. There are now two households where there used to be one. And if one spouse files bankruptcy to get rid of a large amount of jointly acquired debt, it's almost a given that the second spouse will end up filing as well.

I'm not saying you have to share every aspect of your finances with everyone, but when you act guilty, it might be because you are.

9. You let every call go to voice mail.

Well, you're not going to answer the phone yourself, are you? If you do, you're liable to be speaking to a very unpleasant person who wants to know where your payment is. If your heart sinks every time the phone rings, you might want to keep reading this book.

Sometimes, I'll return the phone call of a person who had left me a message seeking information on bankruptcy. I'll get an answering machine and start to leave a message. I'll identify myself as a lawyer returning a call and pause. Suddenly, someone will pick up and say, "Sorry, I thought you were another creditor."

I don't blame them. Some debt collectors are pretty nasty. I've never understood if the people who try to collect debts are naturally obnoxious or they're trained that way. I guess they figure if they are really bad, you'll pay them instead of somebody else just so they don't call back again.

I know I shouldn't slime a whole occupation, but you wouldn't believe the horror stories I've heard. Or maybe you would.

10. You are being sued by a creditor.

This might be the most indicative sign of all. If you get a notice that you are being sued by one of your creditors, you need to consider your options now.

Creditors don't sue people without exhausting their other tactics for getting money out of their customers. Lawsuits cost money. So first they try to harass you into paying. Then they refer the matter to their legal department. Eventually, they'll have to hire a local lawyer to file the case and go to court.

Since you do owe them the money, you might not have a defense to the suit. So it's likely that they'll win and the judge will enter an order that you owe a certain amount of money. Then the creditor can move to collect the debt. It depends on the law in your state, of course, but creditors are frequently allowed to attach bank accounts and garnish wages. This means that your bank or your employer could be ordered to hand over some of your money to your creditor.

Wage garnishment is terrible for two reasons. First, you get a much smaller paycheck than you expected. Second, and perhaps even worse, your employer knows your business. You really don't want everyone at work to know you're having financial problems.

Once a judgment has been entered, your credit is pretty much shot. Paying late is a bad mark on your credit report. Having an account referred to the collections department is another bad mark. The filing of a lawsuit adds another one. Then the judgment makes a bad report even worse.

When you hit this point, it's too late to try to protect your credit report. Now you need to protect what few assets you have from your creditors. Bankruptcy may be the only way to do that.

If you recognized yourself in this chapter, keep reading. In the next chapter, I'll tell you what bankruptcy is and how it may help you make a fresh start.

CHAPTER TWO

WHAT IS BANKRUPTCY?

By any measure, Milton S. Hershey was a successful man. He was born into a family with little money but ended up founding a company that is synonymous with chocolate. However, his first two candy businesses went bankrupt.

But his third attempt focused on a simple milk chocolate bar. That factory expanded to an entire town and a school for orphans. Hershey then built an amusement park for the town and the orphans, later opening it to the world.

Y OU'RE going to hear the words "fresh start" a lot as you learn more about this process. Bankruptcy allows people who are overwhelmed by debt to take a breath and start all over again. It protects the debtor—that's you—from the creditor, the person you owe the money to.

Bankruptcy's origins came from medieval Italy. Merchants had set up shops along the Ponte Vecchio Bridge in Florence. When a merchant couldn't pay his debts, soldiers would come along and destroy his workbench so he wouldn't be able to stay in business. This practice became known as *banco rotto* or "broken bench."

Early forms of bankruptcy were designed to help the creditor, not the debtor. Most cases were involuntary, meaning they were brought by a creditor. By forcing a person into bankruptcy, creditors could at least get something when the debtor's property was sold. The debtor still owed whatever balance might be left and was sometimes thrown in prison if he couldn't pay.

Here in the United States, before there was a United States, the colonies allowed a form of bankruptcy adapted from British law. The procedure varied from colony to colony, some more kind to debtors than others. For example, in some places, debtors were allowed to keep certain property out of the hands of their creditors.

President John Adams signed the first federal bankruptcy law in the U.S. in 1800. Like British versions, it was designed for creditors to use, to force people who couldn't pay their bills into bankruptcy court. Their property was sold and the proceeds divided among the creditors. It was passed in tough economic times, when many people had lost money to land speculation. Once the crisis had passed, the law was repealed in 1803.

Another bankruptcy law was passed in 1841, in response to the panic of 1837. That one lasted only two years before being repealed. After the economic uncertainties brought about by the Civil War, a third federal bankruptcy law was passed in 1867, then repealed in 1878. That version was the first to allow corporations to file for bankruptcy protection.

The Bankruptcy Act of 1898 was the first one to last more than a few years. It was also the first one that focused more on helping the debtor. It allowed debtors to keep more of their property in bankruptcy and it allowed the debts still unpaid to be "discharged," meaning debtors were no longer liable for them.

Let's fast-forward. After many years of tinkering, the bankruptcy law in the twenty-first century is designed to help the debtor start over. Many creditors thought the law too debtor-friendly and managed to get a major rewrite in 2005. Under current law, it is more difficult and more complicated than it once was for people to have their debts erased in bankruptcy.

TYPES OF BANKRUPTCY

THERE ARE several kinds of bankruptcy, depending on who you are and what you want to do. You've probably heard of "Chapter 11"—named for the part of the United States Code where it's located. This applies to corporations that wish to reorganize their finances and remain in business. People with extremely high debts may also be eligible for this kind. There's also a special kind of bankruptcy for family farmers called a "Chapter 12."

There are two kinds of bankruptcy for people, rather than companies and family farmers—the "Chapter 7" and the "Chapter 13." I'll spend three whole chapters discussing the difference, so I won't go into any detail right now. But let me provide a brief explanation.

The theory behind a Chapter 7 is to allow people to liquidate. It's kind of like a going out of business sale for people. People give everything they own to a trustee appointed by the court. The trustees are often bankruptcy lawyers in private practice. Some do this as a small sideline. Others devote much of their time to this work.

The trustee then sells all the property and gives the money to the creditors, as far as it goes. If there's not enough money to pay off the debts, so be it. There is a court order that the debtor no longer owes anything to the creditor and there's nothing the creditor can do about it. This is the discharge order, that the debtor is discharged from any other obligation to pay.

That's the theory. In real life, most people who file a Chapter 7 don't lose anything to the court. That's because although bankruptcy is covered by federal law, state law allows people to keep certain items safe from their creditors. This varies, of course, from state to state.

A Chapter 13 bankruptcy is a way for a person to reorganize the debts. It's like the Chapter 11 that corporations use to avoid going under completely and to keep operating. They are protected from their creditors while working out a way to restructure their financial situation.

Chapter 13 works that way for people. They come up with a plan for paying back their creditors for the next three to five years. The 2005 law requires more people to pay for the longer period. Under this kind of bankruptcy, debtors get to keep their property because they're paying back their creditors.

Bankruptcy law is a relatively modern invention. Be thankful you don't live in a time of workhouses and debtors' prisons!

YOU ARE NOT A CRIMINAL

As an aside, even today I get calls from people worried that falling in debt is a criminal act. They receive a notice that they're being sued by a credit card company and worry that they'll end up in jail. I tell them there are no debtors' prisons in this country and one doesn't go to jail for being poor.

An exception to this is in cases of support. A judge will send a person to jail for failing to pay child or spousal support. The jail term is actually imposed for defying a court order, rather than for not having any money. Similarly, a person may be required to pay a fine or make restitution as part of a criminal case. But those are the only kinds of cases in which jail is a possible punishment for not paying a debt.

That doesn't stop some unscrupulous collection agencies from suggesting otherwise. I've heard of car loan companies threatening to file grand theft auto charges against customers who fell behind in their car payments. I once had an elderly client call me in a panic. She had just been called by a bill collector who insisted that she had to make a payment TODAY. If she didn't, he claimed that he'd send the police to her apartment to lead her away in handcuffs.

Of course he was lying. In fact, he was violating the Fair Debt Collection Practices Act, a law you'll want to learn all about while you're weighing your options. I'll discuss it at some length in chapter nine, Alternatives to Bankruptcy.

Owing money to a credit company is not a crime. But many people don't understand the difference between civil and criminal law. Although I understand why many people feel like criminals when they slink into my office, bankruptcy is a civil proceeding.

THE AUTOMATIC STAY

UNDER EITHER kind of bankruptcy, the creditors must leave you alone immediately. This is something called the "automatic stay." As soon as your bankruptcy petition is filed, there is a "stay" to any actions the creditors might take to try to get you to pay up.

After the stay goes into effect, everything is under the jurisdiction of the bankruptcy court. Creditors must go into bankruptcy court if they believe they have a claim they can still pursue. In Chapter 7 cases, they can object to a debt being discharged for a good reason, such as fraud. In Chapter 13 cases, creditors can raise objections to the way the plan was drafted.

In either case, secured creditors can seek permission to have property repossessed. A secured creditor is someone who loaned you money to buy something—a house or a car, for example. The deal is secured by the property, meaning, if you don't make the payments, the creditor can take back the property. Once the case has been filed, the creditor can't do that without seeking the permission of the court. There are some exceptions, which I'll get to later. The 2005 law makes it easier for secured creditors to regain property in some cases. But generally, creditors may not take any action once a person has filed bankruptcy.

My clients report that bill collectors mostly leave them alone as soon as they find out they're *planning* to file a bankruptcy. I understand the nasty calls suddenly become almost pleasant. This makes no sense at first. Shouldn't the creditors be mad since a bankruptcy may mean they might get nothing?

But think about it a minute. The bill collectors who call on the phone really don't care if you pay. They just want you off their desk. Your filing bankruptcy is an easy way for them to accomplish that goal. All they have to do to close their file on you is to find out information about your bankruptcy case, such as the date it was filed and the case number.

So they call me to confirm that I've been hired to do the job. I say, "Yes, she's retained me. I haven't filed her case yet but I'm working on her papers. Call me back in a few weeks." That's my answer to all creditors for all clients.

The bill collectors are very nice to me. After all, I don't owe their company anything and they're grateful I'll talk to them at all. Many lawyers don't want to deal with creditors until after the bankruptcy is filed.

After that happens, the case winds its way through the process. Most people opt for the Chapter 7 version, which is completed much faster. They attend one hearing to determine whether they have property the court can take and the case is over about three months after it was filed. The court issues a "discharge order" that all their dischargeable debts are discharged, meaning legally wiped away.

It sounds like I'm repeating myself by saying "dischargeable debts are discharged" but I'm not. Not all debts can be discharged in this way, such as child support, student loans, and recent taxes. So the discharge order only applies to debts that may be eliminated under the law.

Chapter 13 cases take much longer. The debtor attends a hearing to determine if his plan to repay the debts is feasible. There may be a second hearing for the judge to approve the plan. The debtor makes his payments for the life of the plan.

In both cases, creditors may raise objections with the court. But they have no choice but to accept whatever the court decides is appropriate for you.

———————•———————

CHAPTER THREE

TAKING AN HONEST LOOK AT YOUR SITUATION

Abraham Lincoln is considered one of our greatest presidents. But he had many setbacks and failures before he was elected in 1860. He ran for the Illinois legislature in 1832 and lost. That same year he lost a job and failed to get into law school. So in 1833 he borrowed some money from a friend and opened up a general store, which failed by the end of the year. But Honest Abe paid back his creditors anyway. It took him seventeen years.

O KAY, this is it. I understand that you've been going through a very rough time. You haven't wanted to open the bills, to add stuff up. You knew, you just knew, that you were going to get out of this mess somehow if you kept working hard. There was really no need to look at the big picture, was there? And you've been too busy trying to dig yourself out anyway.

The most important thing you can do right now for your financial future is to figure out exactly how bad things are. I happen to be of the opinion that it's always better to know than not to know. When I have to have blood drawn, I'd rather watch the needle than close my eyes. Okay, I admit that's a little weird. But my point is that reality is often not as bad as what your vivid imagination can conjure up.

Yes, bankruptcy may be in your future. That's why you picked up this book. But it may not be. You may find that your situation is not that bad and some other option will get you out of your financial hole. But you must first figure out how deep that hole is. Follow the simple rules in this chapter, and you'll soon know.

1. Open unopened bills.

If you're like some of my clients, the very first step might be to open your mail. You might have dozens of unopened bills scattered about your home and stuffed into drawers. Gather them all up in a pile on the kitchen table. Don't be discouraged by the size of the pile.

2. Organize the bills.

If you really have been in denial for months, you may have a lot of duplicates. I used to say you could safely toss the extra ones but now you might need any communication you received from a creditor in the past ninety days. You can get rid of the really old ones.

But be sure that anything you throw out is truly a duplicate. It's not unusual for one person to have three different credit cards from the same bank. Double-check the account numbers before you throw out what appears to be an older statement for the same account.

You might not even know what some of the bills represent. After a creditor gets tired of harassing you, it may hire a collection agency or an attorney to do the dirty work. Somewhere on the statement it should say who their client is. If you do have collection agencies or attorneys involved, you'll want to have a list of all of them. If you end up filing bankruptcy, you'll want to make sure everybody gets a notice.

When I file a bankruptcy, I list the original creditor in that part of the paperwork that lists all the debts. I also make sure that any collection agency or attorney is part of the mailing matrix that lists everyone who will get a notice. Creditors change these collection agencies all the time, so you might get two or three notices from different companies on the same debt. Make sure you keep some statement from all the collection agencies as well as all the creditors.

3. Set aside bills for regular expenses.

For this purpose, you don't want to include in your overall debt pile those regular expenses such as your phone bill or your car insurance. Put those aside in a separate stack. You'll need them later.

4. Assess your debts by filling out Worksheet 1 on page 135.

Use this worksheet to make a history of all the bills you have collected. Be sure to read the fine print to find out what interest rate you're being charged. You'll also have to figure out what part of your payment is going toward paying down the principal part of the debt, rather than being eaten up by interest.

Add up the balances, then take a deep breath. It's quite likely to be a higher number than you had in your head. Unfortunately, your head can't keep track of all the late fees, interest, over-limit penalties, etc. It's amazing how quickly a $2,000 credit card bill can turn into a $3,000 one when you're not paying attention.

Then write down a grand total of that part of the minimum payments that goes to the principal. Divide the debt total by that to get an idea of how many months it would take you to pay back the debts at that rate.

There is nothing magical about this process. You can be more detailed or less detailed, depending on your proclivities. The idea is for you to get a realistic idea of how much you owe and how long it would take for you to pay it back.

5. Figure out exactly how much money you make, by filling out Worksheet 2: Monthly Income on page 136.

This can be easy or tricky, depending on your situation. Some people get the same amount in their checks every payday. Others have amounts that vary wildly. It may depend on the number of hours they work, such as overtime. Some people work on commission, so they might get a big fat check one time and nothing much the next.

Even if you get paid the same amount in every check, every other week, be aware that you still need to come up with a monthly figure. Getting paid every other week is a bit more than two paychecks per month, since there are twenty-six pay periods every year instead of twenty-four. So take the amount of a single paycheck and multiply by twenty-six to get a yearly figure. Then divide the annual amount by twelve to get a monthly figure.

You'll have to get a bit more creative if your check varies greatly from week to week. If you can, reconstruct your pay for the last six months and then divide by six to get an amount per month. Most paychecks also provide a year-to-date figure that you can use to determine your monthly income so far in the current year.

Right now, this doesn't have to be exact, down to the penny. But it will be very helpful for you in your decision-making to have a realistic idea of how much money you're bringing home each month. Make sure you consider all income from all sources, such as child support, government assistance, and the occasional odd job.

If you do decide you may need to file bankruptcy, you *will* need to be as exact as possible. The 2005 law prevents some people from filing a Chapter 7 bankruptcy based on their income. And income is defined as the average over a six-month period. I'll get into more detail on that later.

6. Calculate your basic monthly expenses by filling out Worksheet 3 on page 137.

This is where your stack of bills for regular expenses becomes useful. Try to think of everything that you regularly have to pay. You might have trouble in this area, but do the best you can.

For example, if you've been sticking all your grocery purchases on credit cards in the last few months, you might not even know the actual prices of things these days. If you truly have no idea, go to the store and write down your regular items and the prices. I know it sounds silly, but the whole idea is to get as realistic a view as possible of what it takes to keep your family alive.

Don't forget those mundane items that add up, such as soap and toilet paper. Some categories may vary over the course of a year, such as electricity. Do what you did with your income and try to figure out a monthly figure by examining the bills over the last several months. You could carry a notebook around with you for a while and write down everything you spend, even down to the newspaper at the bus stop and the soft drink from the machine at work.

While you're figuring out your actual expenses, you might spot areas where you can cut back. You could start a separate list of those. If it turns out you think you can avoid bankruptcy, you'll want to devote every dollar you can to paying down your debt.

7. Calculate your assets by filling out Worksheet 4 on page 139.

Similarly, if you find you can avoid bankruptcy, you might be able to raise cash by selling off some assets. So make a list of everything you own and the approximate value. You might have overlooked some asset that could help you get out of this mess.

For example, I've had clients who didn't realize they had a "whole life" life insurance policy until I asked the question and they looked for the answer. This is not the "term life" kind you get through your job but an investment that can attain some cash value in time. If you find some papers on a life insurance policy, call up the company and ask if the policy has any "cash surrender" value.

I'm not suggesting you cash out or sell anything at this point. In fact, it's probably better that you hold off and don't make any decisions at all in these information-gathering days. You need to assemble all your facts before you even think about taking any action.

I'm a lawyer, not a shrink, but I do believe that one of the greatest side effects of this organizing process is psychological. Sure, you'll get a sinking feeling in the pit of your stomach when you see the grand total of debts. You might want to burst into tears when you see the extent of your cash flow problem.

But at least you are doing something. You're not just sitting around worrying; you're being proactive. You are taking charge of your own problem and you're taking the first step toward a better financial future. You've got to know exactly where you stand before you can begin to figure out how to get where you want to go.

For example, look at the total amount of debt. Then look at your budget and decide realistically how much money you could devote each month to paying it off. Divide the total amount of debt by the monthly amount you could pay to find out how many months it would take to pay off the debt. Of course this doesn't take into account the extra interest, but it will give you a very rough idea.

If it appears that you could pay off the debt in a reasonable amount of time, it would probably be better if you did not file bankruptcy. But if it appears that it would take you several years, even with devoting every dollar to the effort, you should consider other options. Your situation is getting worse every day.

CHAPTER FOUR

FREQUENTLY ASKED QUESTIONS ABOUT BANKRUPTCY

Before the name "Heinz" was associated with ketchup, Henry John Heinz had a company that sold sauerkraut, as well as pickles, vinegar, and horseradish. It didn't do well and he had to file bankruptcy in 1875.

So Heinz started another company that made a new product he called ketchup. That one caught on.

Now that you've reviewed your situation, you might want to explore the idea of bankruptcy. Most people know little or nothing about the process, except what they've understood or misunderstood from friends or relatives.

Here are some of the questions that come up most often in my practice.

Q: *Will my employer know about my filing bankruptcy?*

A: Not unless you owe your employer money—only creditors are notified about your filing. Of course, if you belong to a credit union at work, those people will know about it. That information shouldn't drift out of the credit union office and into your part of the building.

But your employer might learn your bankruptcy status if you actually get sued. Once there's a judgment against you from a lawsuit, a creditor can sometimes, depending on your state's laws, get your wages attached. This means the creditor can get a court to require your employer to withhold part of your wages to pay the debt. At that point, your employer would know that you're having financial trouble. But that's actually an argument *in favor of* bankruptcy. If you can file before things get this bad, your employer won't have to know what's going on because you'll be protected against such judgments.

Q: *Can I be turned down for a government job because of a bankruptcy?*

A: Under federal law, the government cannot refuse to hire you solely because you filed bankruptcy. This also applies to state and local governments. But I'm not going to tell you that it never happens.

You just can't tell what is in a person's head and, although such discrimination is against the law, how can you prove that you were turned down for that reason? The person denying you the job would need to signal in some unambiguous way that your bankruptcy was the reason you were denied employment.

Governments are also prohibited from cutting off benefits or denying licenses to people who have filed bankruptcy, if the bankruptcy was the only reason for the denial. In my state, people can lose their driver's licenses if there's a driving-related judgment against them. They can't pay for the accident, so they end up filing bankruptcy as the only way to get their licenses back.

In the private sector, employers may not fire you solely because you've filed bankruptcy. But the law is unclear on whether they can safely refuse to hire you. And they'll probably find out about it.

Potential employers have the right to pull your credit report as part of their check into your background. For some jobs, a bad credit rating is a drawback because it is relevant to the job itself—for example, a job like bank teller, or cashier, or one involving access to sensitive documents. Someone with a lot of debt may be tempted to steal or accept a bribe in order to pick up some extra cash.

Although filing for bankruptcy means you no longer owe any money, and that you would therefore be a *good* security risk, apparently not everyone sees it this way. Again, I doubt they'd tell you that the bankruptcy was the reason you didn't get the job.

Q: *Will my name be published in the newspaper?*

A: Not necessarily, and probably not at all. It could happen if you live in a very small town with an aggressive local paper that scours the local court filings. Bankruptcy *is* a matter of public record, and anyone can stroll down to the local courthouse and peruse the filings.

In most cases, though, people don't care. I practice bankruptcy law in a large, metropolitan area, and only large companies make the paper when they file for bankruptcy. Hundreds of ordinary people file every week and escape public attention. That is most likely to happen in your case.

Q: *Will the court turn me down for bankruptcy? Is there a certain amount of debt you must have?*

A: No, there is no minimum level of debt. Of course, if the amount is so small that it's close to the cost of filing, the court might decide that a filing would be an abuse of the system—that, in other words, you've simply decided that you'd rather pay the lawyer than the creditor.

The court could also dismiss your case if you lie, don't show up for your hearing, or otherwise don't cooperate. Fraud is another reason to dismiss your case—for example, if you hide assets. But if you are completely honest with your lawyer and tell the court everything, there should be no problem.

Q: *Will I be forced to close my bank account?*

A: The court doesn't close your bank account, but you might want to. If you have a credit card with your bank, the bank might freeze your account before you have a chance to file bankruptcy. Also, if you owe your bank as a result of overdraft protection, you have to list the account as a creditor anyway. Under those circumstances, you'd be better off shutting down the account and opening up a new one at a bank where you don't have any connection.

If your bank is not a creditor, you don't have to list it as a creditor, and you don't run the risk that the banker will snatch your money. But you will have to list whatever cash is in the account as part of your property at the time you file.

Q: *Can my creditors stop me from filing for bankruptcy?*

A: No. We have evolved beyond the days when creditors could have their debtors imprisoned or force them to work off their debts. You have a *right* to file for bankruptcy protection, and no creditor can prevent you from doing it. An individual creditor can object to a particular debt being discharged. A typical reason is fraud. If you charge a European vacation on your American Express card a week before you file, American Express is going to object.

Also, if you lied outrageously on your credit card application, a creditor can object, saying that it wouldn't have given you the card if it had known the truth. But your creditor has to have a strong case. The burden is on the creditor to prove that the debt should not be discharged, rather than on you to prove that it should.

As a practical matter, creditors don't usually object unless there's a lot of money involved. They have to pay a filing fee to object and hire a lawyer in your particular jurisdiction. It must be worth the time and money to pursue a claim.

Q: *What does it cost to file bankruptcy?*

A: As of this writing, the filing fee that goes to the bankruptcy court is $274 for a Chapter 7 and $189 for a Chapter 13. That's just what's paid to the court. There may also be a small fee to the county court where you live to protect your property.

The cost of hiring a lawyer can vary widely, depending on where you live and how complicated your case may be. Some attorneys charge a flat rate, meaning it's a set amount no matter how long it takes for the lawyer to do the work. Others charge by the hour. I can't even give you a range of what it might cost because the range would be so wide, it wouldn't be helpful. It could be just a few hundred dollars if you live in a depressed area or it could be in the thousands.

This area of the law tends to be rather competitive so you're not likely to find that big a range where you live. It shouldn't take too many phone calls to estimate the going rate in your area. But don't go by price alone. Turn to chapter ten for more suggestions about hiring a bankruptcy lawyer.

Q: *Is it true that I won't be allowed to get a credit card again for ten years?*

A: No, it's not true. First of all, there's no rule on what you can do. The bankruptcy covers all debts incurred before the filing. After the filing, you can go out and incur any new debt you want. Of course, it's a matter of finding creditors willing to extend you credit. Some won't want to deal with you. Others will. And some will actively seek your business. You're actually a good credit risk right after the bankruptcy. You don't have any debt, and under the 2005 law, you can't file for bankruptcy protection again for eight years. (It used to be six years.)

I've even had some repeat business, clients who came back to me for a second bankruptcy. Some were waiting for the time to be up so they could file again. I don't recommend that, of course, but it does demonstrate how much credit trouble you can get into in only six years. Of course sometimes there are circumstances beyond one's control—such as a job loss or an uninsured illness.

Q: *I don't want to include my car loan in the bankruptcy. I need my car to get to work and can't risk losing it.*

A: First, you can't play favorites. That's one of the big rules in bankruptcy. You can't just list the debts you want to get rid of, and not mention the others. But you can voluntarily repay anyone you want after you file the bankruptcy.

This happens all the time with car loans, and it is something called "reaffirmation." Reaffirmation is a separate contract to "re-affirm" the debt with the car loan company. The terms are usually the same as for the original loan. Everyone signs it—you, the car loan people, and your lawyer—and it gets filed with the court. Then it's like the bankruptcy never happened, as far as the car loan is concerned.

You won't lose your car to the court, unless it is worth more than you are allowed to keep in your state—and it is probably *not*, if you're still paying it off. Cars depreciate fairly quickly. In fact, lots of cars are "under water," meaning you owe more than the thing is worth. That's good for you in this regard. If the bankruptcy trustee took your car as part of a Chapter 7 filing, he or she would have to pay off the car loan first and then resell the car to raise funds for your other creditors. After selling a car that is "under water," there would be nothing left for the trustee to give to the rest of the creditors. So the trustee is probably not going to care about your car, and it's up to you whether you want to keep it and keep paying on it.

Sometimes, in fact, people in a Chapter 7 will take this opportunity to get out of a bad car deal. They decide to give the car back instead of reaffirming the debt. They then owe nothing, even if the outstanding balance is higher than the value of the car. The creditor cannot try to collect the difference.

Another option for your car is to pay the car loan company only what it's worth, rather than the full amount of the outstanding balance. This is called "redemption"; in effect you're buying it from the lender. But you'd have to pay it in a lump sum and most people can't do that.

There are some companies that offer special loans for this purpose. But be very careful. Read the fine print. It could be they'll charge you such a high interest rate that you'd be better off with the original deal.

Q: *Will my landlord be told I'm filing bankruptcy, and if so, will I be evicted?*

A: If you are obligated under a lease, you will have to disclose your landlord's name and address in your bankruptcy schedules. The court wants to know where your money is obligated. But the court will not notify him.

An exception to this is if you want to leave the apartment and not owe anything on the balance of the lease. You should then list the landlord among your creditors and be prepared to move as soon as possible. The broken lease would be discharged along with the rest of your creditors.

If you stay and continue to pay your rent, the landlord can't evict you. Even if you don't pay, he can't evict you during the bankruptcy unless he gets the permission of the court or if he got an eviction order before you filed.

Unless you're in a very expensive lease that you want to escape, you might want to stay put. You could have a problem finding a new place. Sometimes landlords don't want to rent to people with a bankruptcy on their records. And, if you faithfully pay your rent on time, you'll have one good credit reference to show a future landlord.

Q: *I'm having financial problems now, but I expect to make more money in a year or so. If I file a Chapter 7, can the creditors or the bankruptcy court come back in the future and say that I should now have to pay the debts?*

A: No. Everything the court decides is based on your financial circumstances on the day that you file. You list all your debts, assets, income, and expenses as of that date. The income is based on the previous six months. You'll also have to say if you expect an income change (either higher or lower) of ten percent in the next six months. You tell the court if that's the case. But otherwise, the only thing that matters is the truth as of the day you file. Once you file, everything is under the jurisdiction of the court. Unless the creditor can prove in court that a particular debt shouldn't be discharged, the creditor can do nothing.

It's a little different in Chapter 13 cases. Your trustee will want to see annual reports of any changes in income that would allow you to devote more money to the plan. Under the 2005 law, any "party of interest" can demand you file an updated tax return. This means one of your creditors could force you to provide details that could lead to you having to increase the monthly payment. This change is too new to know if many creditors will do this.

Just make sure you make all your payments on time. You don't want to give anybody any reason to pay attention to you.

Q: *Will my creditors tell anyone that I filed bankruptcy, such as the relative I had to put down on my credit application?*

A: They shouldn't, and I've never heard of that happening. While this can feel like a very personal experience to you, keep reminding yourself that this is just a business transaction to most of your creditors. Typically, creditors simply write you off when they get the notice that you filed bankruptcy. They don't waste any more time on you.

They're not allowed to contact you again or try to get you to pay. In fact, your attorney might argue, if the creditor were to rat you out to your mother or even threaten to do so, that they were trying to pressure you—in violation of a court order protecting you—to pay. Creditors will get in trouble with the court if they don't abide by the automatic stay.

Q: *I am still legally married but have lived apart from my husband for two years. Can I file by myself, or do I have to file jointly with my husband?*

A: You can file by yourself, and that would be the case *even* if you were still living together. However, if you are listing joint debts, the creditors can then go after your husband for payment. If there is a lot of joint debt, it might make sense for both parties to file together, even if they aren't living together. For one thing, filing one joint bankruptcy petition would be less expensive than filing two separately. But you can only file together if you are still legally married.

If you're thinking about divorce, you ought to consult with a domestic relations attorney in your area to discuss how a bankruptcy would affect your case. Make sure your bankruptcy lawyer knows about your divorce. You may have to list your husband as a creditor. He should know, in any event, since he could be affected if you have joint property or joint debts. You should never try to hide a bankruptcy from your spouse or the family court.

Q: *I have one credit card that my father cosigned on. If I file for bankruptcy, can that debt be discharged?*

A: It will be discharged for you, but not for your dad, unless he also files for bankruptcy protection. You have to list it, but you can voluntarily pay it later to keep him from getting stuck with it.

In the bankruptcy papers, you have to put down his name and address, in the part that asks about codebtors. This puts creditors on notice that there is someone else they can go after for the debt. As long as it's being paid, your father shouldn't be bothered. Creditors don't care who sends the money as long as someone does.

Q: *I already have a judgment against me. Is it too late for me to file?*

A: No, the judgment can be included in the bankruptcy. The creditor can't try to collect the debt after the filing, even if there has been a judgment entered. But you need to make sure your lawyer knows about the judgment so that it is included in your petition for protection. He or she may have to file papers with the court where the judgment was entered to show that the judgment can't be enforced.

It *is* probably better, whenever possible, to file before the judgment is entered. Once there is a judgment, it can show up on a credit report even after the bankruptcy. Although the creditor can't collect, the judgment *did* happen. If you file bankruptcy before the judgment is entered, then your credit report will just show the bankruptcy, not a bankruptcy and a judgment.

Q: *Will I have to appear in court?*

A: There is at least one hearing you will have to go to. It is called a "creditor's meeting" because your creditors can show up and ask you questions about your debts and assets. The vast majority of creditors don't bother. You will be asked questions by a bankruptcy trustee, who is not a judge but a lawyer appointed to look into your case.

In Chapter 7 cases, the trustee will be mainly looking for assets to sell. For most people, this hearing before the trustee is the only court proceeding that they have to attend. The trustee will also be looking to see if you meet the new income requirements for filing that kind of bankruptcy.

In Chapter 13 cases, the trustee will be examining your plan to see if it will work. Also, depending on where you live, you may have to attend a confirmation hearing when the plan is actually approved. Some courts require the appearance of the debtor at a confirmation hearing. Others schedule a hearing on whether to confirm the plan only if an objection has been raised by the trustee or one of the creditors.

Q: *Will I be lectured to about my poor spending habits? I don't think I want to go through this if I'm going to be scolded in public.*

A: There is always the possibility that you'll have a particularly cranky trustee. But most trustees treat the creditor's meeting as a routine procedure. Most don't care why you got into this situation. They want just the facts. In Chapter 7 cases, they want to know if you have any property they can take or if your income makes you ineligible. The Chapter 13 trustee wants to know if your payment plan is feasible.

If you think it would be especially traumatic for you to be treated harshly by the trustee, ask your lawyer about the trustees in your jurisdiction. But I think you ought to suck it up. If bankruptcy is the right option for you, you shouldn't turn it down just because you might experience a few minutes of unpleasantness.

Q: *How do I know for sure if bankruptcy is the right thing for me to do?*

A: I can't tell you that. This is your case, and it is your decision. Read everything you can and find a lawyer you can work with. And ask every question on your mind. This is a business decision, not a moral one. Look at all your options as clearly as you can. And remember that a bankruptcy is just one stop along the road to improving your financial situation.

PART TWO

WEIGHING YOUR OPTIONS

CHAPTER FIVE

"CHAPTER 7"—
THE LIQUIDATION
BANKRUPTCY

Kim Basinger made so much money playing the love interest in Batman, *she was able to form an investment group to buy her hometown of Braselton, Georgia, for a cool $20 million. Her good fortune didn't last. Four years later, Main Line Pictures sued her and won a judgment for $8.1 million because she backed out of a commitment to star in a movie called* Boxing Helena.

Basinger had to sell her interest in Braselton for $1 million and filed for bankruptcy protection. But life went on and she won an Oscar for her performance in L.A. Confidential *in 1997.*

CHAPTER 7, DEFINED

THE CHAPTER 7 is a going-out-of-business sale for people. The idea is that you give all your property to the bankruptcy court. The bankruptcy trustee sells it and then distributes the money to the creditors, as far as it goes. After the money is gone, the creditors get nothing.

That's the idea. But most people don't lose anything in a Chapter 7 bankruptcy. Bankruptcy is governed by federal law, while every state has its own rules about what property a person is entitled to keep safe from creditors. Such laws are called "homestead exemptions."

HOMESTEAD EXEMPTIONS

THESE LAWS vary widely. For example, some states, such as Florida, Kansas, and Texas, allow you to keep your home, no matter how expensive it is. There may be limitations on the number of acres you can keep, but there is no dollar limit in most cases.

I say "in most cases" because the 2005 law did put some limitations on how much one can claim no matter what the state says. For example, the homestead exemption is now limited to $125,000 if the property was bought within 1,215 days of the filing of the bankruptcy petition. (No, I don't know where they got that number.) The limit is also $125,000 if a court determines that the debtor had, within five years, committed certain crimes, such as racketeering. But outside of certain exceptions, debtors in a few states can keep even an expensive home.

Most other states aren't so generous. Massachusetts allows the debtor to keep a house worth $300,000. It's $50,000 in Idaho and $5,000 in South Carolina. The value of the house is calculated by figuring out the current market value and then deducting any loans against it, such as mortgages and equity loans.

Since a house is usually the most valuable property anyone owns, that is likely to be a major factor in whether you decide to file a Chapter 7 bankruptcy, rather than a Chapter 13.

But even if you don't have a house to consider, you must figure out if you have anything valuable to lose in a Chapter 7 bankruptcy in your state.

The various state laws actually itemize the different kinds of property, such as cars, household furnishings, and retirement accounts. Some states also have a catchall, "wildcard" category for things of value that don't fit anywhere else, such as cash and jewelry. In some states, that's where the equity of your house is listed as well.

And then there are states with categories for things that many people don't have. Michigan, for example, allows people to keep "10 sheep, 2 cows, 5 swine, 100 hens, 5 roosters, and a six-month supply of feed." Iowa allows debtors to hang on to their shotgun and either their musket or their rifle, no matter how expensive the firearms may be. West Virginia protects "unripe crops" from creditors.

Turn to the list in Appendix II, page 141 to get an idea of what the states allow you to keep in your house and in the wildcard category, if there is one. This list does not tell the whole story. Some states provide a higher amount if you are in a special category such as disabled veteran or over the age of sixty-five. Some don't let you use the excess in one category to cover a shortfall in the other. You need to consult an attorney in your state or at least look up the exemptions in your state law.

HOW CHAPTER 7 WORKS

HERE'S HOW it works in a Chapter 7 bankruptcy case. Your lawyer draws up the papers, based on the information you provided. They're called "the schedules" because the papers are divided into "Schedule A," "Schedule B," etc., as an organizational tool. Check out an example in Appendix V on page 155.

You review the papers very carefully to make sure everything is accurate and you understand everything. You sign it in several places. Remember, you are signing these papers under penalty of perjury, so if there is anything out of order, now is the time to speak up. The case is filed, which triggers the automatic stay, so that you're under the protection of the bankruptcy court.

Perhaps about a month after you file, you will have to attend a hearing. It's called a creditor's meeting, because it's a chance for your creditors to ask you questions about your debts and assets. But not many creditors show up.

The main purpose of the hearing will be for a trustee to question you to determine if you have any assets to take and sell to raise cash for your creditors. This is usually a fairly routine matter. Your lawyer should be able to tell if there's anything unusual about your case.

If all goes well, you'll receive a discharge order about two months after the hearing. This order means that you are discharged from paying your debts. The creditors may no longer attempt to collect them.

WHO IS ELIGIBLE FOR CHAPTER 7?

THE BIGGEST change brought about by the 2005 law was that it disqualified many people from filing a Chapter 7 bankruptcy—many people who make more than the median income in their states. And it's not a simple matter to figure out whether you are ineligible. I'll go into detail on that in chapter seven, where I'll discuss how to decide between the kinds of bankruptcy.

Other people are also ineligible for a Chapter 7 discharge; for example, those who already received a discharge in a Chapter 7 case within the previous eight years. People who had a bankruptcy case dismissed within the previous 180 days are also ineligible for a Chapter 7 discharge if the case was dismissed on certain grounds, such as refusing to show up for their hearing.

DEBTS BANKRUPTCY WILL NOT ERASE

THERE ARE debts that, as a matter of law, cannot be discharged in bankruptcy, including child and spousal support, criminal fines, and debts that arose as the result of drunken driving. Student loans are also excluded from a discharge. Congress decided that people who were getting a special deal to borrow money to go to school shouldn't be able to wiggle out of the obligation later on.

There is a way to get a student loan discharged in bankruptcy but it doesn't happen very often. You'd have to go into bankruptcy court separately and ask the judge to grant you a hardship discharge. You have to show that paying back the loan would impose an "undue hardship" on you and your dependents.

This is not an easy thing to do. A person in bankruptcy court is almost by definition a person with little money. To get this special treatment, you'd have to demonstrate that you wouldn't be able to maintain even a minimal standard of living. You'd also have to show that the hardship would continue for most of the life of the loan. And you'd have to be able to prove that you made a good-faith effort to pay back the money.

This is not an easy case to make. Certainly, you wouldn't want to go into a court without a lawyer to do the arguing. But if you could afford to hire a lawyer, you'd be undermining your own case.

TAXES

TAXES ARE another debt that often can't be discharged. The rules on discharging taxes in bankruptcy are too complicated to explain thoroughly here. Whole books have been written on the subject. All-day seminars discuss the details. But here is a simplified version.

Income taxes may be discharged under three conditions:

1. The taxes must be at least three years old, meaning they were due at least three years before you filed your petition. That date is usually April 15 of the year following the tax year.

2. The taxes must have actually been filed at least two years before you file the bankruptcy.

3. The third condition is that at least 240 days have passed since the taxes were assessed, meaning that the Internal Revenue Service decided exactly what you owe.

You might know the first two dates but you're unlikely to know this one. If you owe taxes that you think might be discharged, it's a good idea to get a copy of your transcript from the I.R.S. to be sure of all the dates. You can request a transcript from your local I.R.S. office.

Even if the tax debt meets all of the above conditions, it still won't be discharged if the I.R.S. can show that the return was fraudulently filed or that you willfully tried to evade the tax or committed tax fraud, such as hiding income or using a phony Social Security number.

FRAUD

CONSUMER DEBTS won't be discharged if they were obtained by fraud. In this situation, it would be up to the creditor to object to a certain debt being discharged and they'd have to complain before the discharge order is entered. That doesn't happen very often. I'll discuss that in chapter seventeen.

———— • ————

CHAPTER SIX

"CHAPTER 13"—THE "WAGE-EARNER'S" PLAN

The writer Samuel Clemens, known as Mark Twain, filed bankruptcy in 1894. Part of the reason was a bad investment. He sunk a good bit of his money in something called a "Paige Compositer," an automatic typesetting machine that never performed as promised.

Although his debts were discharged, Twain was determined to pay them anyway. He went out on the road, lecturing in Europe as well as the United States. Eventually, he paid all his creditors and continued to write.

CHAPTER 13, DEFINED

CHAPTER 13 is like those "Chapter 11" bankruptcies you hear about on the news, except it is for people rather than corporations. It's a reorganization plan, to allow you to catch your breath, and then carry on. It's called a "wage-earner's" plan because it requires the person who files it to have some source of income to carry it out.

The idea is that for a certain period of time, you turn over all your disposable income to the bankruptcy trustee. The typical time period used to be three years but now more people will be required to pay for five years. The trustee then pays your creditors. By "disposable income," I mean anything you make that isn't spent on the basic necessities—such as food, shelter, and transportation. There are even guidelines to follow on what you should be spending in relation to your income. A court will reject your plan if you seem too extravagant.

This kind of bankruptcy is also like one of those consumer credit counseling plans I'll talk about in the section on bankruptcy alternatives, except the creditors have to accept what they get. The bankruptcy filing protects you from any lawsuits, harassment, etc.

HOW CHAPTER 13 DIFFERS FROM CHAPTER 7

A MAJOR difference from the Chapter 7 bankruptcy is that you get to keep all your property. You don't lose anything to the court since your creditors are getting paid. So if you own a house with a lot of equity, and you live in most states where you are limited in the amount of home equity you can keep, you might want to do a Chapter 13 to keep your house.

In deciding whether to approve a Chapter 13 plan, the courts will look at what might happen if the debtor filed a Chapter 7 instead. Say the debtor has a house with a lot of equity in it, well above what that particular state allows a debtor to keep. If the debtor wants to file a Chapter 13 to keep the house, the total amount going to the creditors over the life of the plan must be at least as much as the creditors would get if the house were sold and the proceeds divvied up in a Chapter 7.

Ideally, in a Chapter 13 you would be able to come up with a 100 percent plan, meaning you would end up paying your creditors in full. But that might not be possible. Courts will approve a less than 100 percent plan, if it turns out that the creditors would do better than if you filed a Chapter 7.

That kind of calculation is one of many you need to do in deciding which kind of bankruptcy is best for you.

Another major consideration is your income in relation to your expenses. If you want the court to approve your plan, you have to show you can afford to follow it. You also want to show the court that you are devoting every available dollar to the effort.

By now you should have a pretty accurate idea of how much money is coming in and going out of your household each month. If that amount is about the same, or your expenses are greater than your income, you can't do a Chapter 13. You have to be able to show your plan is realistic.

If your plan calls for something less than a 100 percent payback to the creditors, the outstanding balances of many debts would be discharged if the court approves the plan and you make all the required payments. The discharge would not apply to some debts, such as student loans and child support.

The plan will last from three to five years, depending on your situation. Again, the details of the plan are left up to you. But the trustee will object if it's not reasonable.

Here's another reason why it's usually best to hire an experienced bankruptcy lawyer. He or she will know what is considered realistic in your jurisdiction. The main person you have to please is the bankruptcy trustee in charge of your case. Some are pickier than others. A lawyer who does a lot of Chapter 13 bankruptcies in your area will be familiar with the trustees and will know what would be accepted and what would be rejected. You need to know what will fly before you file. In fact, you should know what works in your area before you decide if you should file.

WHO IS ELIGIBLE?

THE FIRST thing your lawyer will do is to decide if you are eligible for a Chapter 13. You must be an individual (rather than a company) with regular income. This does not mean that only people with salaried jobs may file. This option is also available to people who are self-employed or are living on a pension. The trick is to show that the income is regular and stable enough to pay for the plan.

There is a limitation on the amount of debt owed by a person in Chapter 13. As of this writing, your unsecured debts must be less than $307,675. Your secured debts must be less than $922,975. If you owe more than those limits, you may be able to file a Chapter 11 bankruptcy, just like a corporation.

You might not be sure what kind of debts you have. With a secured debt, the creditor can take some property back if you don't pay, for example, foreclose on your house or repossess your car. Unsecured debts don't have any collateral attached to them, for example, your normal credit cards or medical bills.

Besides limits on the debt, you may not file a Chapter 13 if you are either a stockbroker or a commodity broker. And within the previous 180 days, you must not have had another bankruptcy case dismissed on certain grounds, such as violating an order of the court.

HOW CHAPTER 13 WORKS

In a Chapter 13 bankruptcy, be prepared to stay in close contact with your lawyer. He or she will need lots of information from you, so be as complete and accurate as you can. You'll have to file a complete petition, just like in a Chapter 7, but you'll also file the plan detailing how you plan to pay your creditors. Ideally, they're filed at the same time, but sometimes debtors aren't ready with the plan right away. The plan must be filed within fifteen days of the filing of the petition or your case will be dismissed.

You must make your first payment within thirty days of filing the plan. So even if the plan has not been accepted yet, you must start the payment process. Many jurisdictions require that you make your payment by a direct allotment through your employer.

That's probably a good idea even if it's not required where you live. If the money is gone before you get your paycheck, you won't ever fall behind. Most Chapter 13 bankruptcies fail because people can't keep up the payments.

Of course this might mean your employer will know about the bankruptcy. You'll have to direct your payroll office to take a certain amount from your paycheck and send it to the trustee. If the trustee wants the check sent to "Ebenezer Scrooge, Chapter 13 Trustee," your employer will figure it out. But remember: there is nothing shameful about getting your finances in order.

When the creditors receive the notice that you've filed, they submit a "proof of claim" with the court. It's a statement of what they think you owe them. It may be higher than you expected. Keep this in mind when you're considering whether you have the ability to carry out a payment plan. You don't want to get into this thing and find out that it won't work.

About a month after you file, you must attend a hearing before the trustee who was appointed to handle your case. In chapter fifteen, I'll go into detail on what happens at the hearing, but generally, the idea is for the trustee to see if your plan is workable. This might be the time for the trustee to challenge some of your expenses so be prepared to show documentation on them, if necessary.

You'll probably find out at the hearing (but not before) if the trustee has any major problems and you'll have a chance to rework your plan to meet any objections. Nothing happens quickly in bankruptcy court and you usually have time to make changes. Again, it's the trustee you need to please. The court is likely to confirm any plan that makes the trustee happy.

Some courts require that the debtors appear at the confirmation hearing as well. Other courts don't schedule a confirmation hearing unless an objection has been raised.

After the judge has confirmed the plan, all you need to do is make your payments on time. After all the payments are made, the bankruptcy is over.

—————————— • ——————————

DECIDING BETWEEN CHAPTER 7 AND CHAPTER 13

In August 2004, Donald Trump announced that his company, Trump Hotels &
Casinos Resorts, was filing for bankruptcy—again. He told Fox TV that the de-
cision was not a failure, but will lead to success, that he's creating a terrific com-
pany, that it makes him "feel very good." In fact, his company emerged from
bankruptcy the following April.

    He had filed bankruptcies for three casinos he owned in 1992, listing more
than $1 billion in debt. By 1997, he was a billionaire again, a journey he de-
tailed in a book Trump: The Art of the Comeback.

AN ADMISSION OF BIAS

I MUST admit to you that I'm biased in favor of Chapter 7. In fact, I don't usually recommend a Chapter 13 unless it's clear to me the client couldn't be squeezed into a
Chapter 7. Other lawyers are biased the other way and recommend a Chapter 7 only
if it's clear that a Chapter 13 can't be done.

    Let me explain my thinking. The whole purpose of any kind of bankruptcy is to move through it to the other side and get your financial life back on track. A Chapter 7 fulfills that goal a whole lot faster. You can start over again almost immediately, rather than three to five years down the road.

Sure, filing a Chapter 13 may be seen as less negative to creditors in the future than filing a Chapter 7. But I'm not sure that advantage is enough to make it worthwhile. Lots of creditors just see the "B" word and that's enough for them. I don't think most creditors know enough about the difference between the two to affect their decisions. Face it—you're going to have a bad mark on your credit report for several years, regardless of which version you choose.

BUT DO YOU HAVE A CHOICE?

BANKRUPTCY LAW now forces more people to choose a Chapter 13. In the past, if you didn't have any property to lose, you could file a Chapter 7 without attracting any attention. Of course, judges always have had the power to dismiss a case if it's found to be an abuse of the system. For example, if you have a great income and few expenses, the court is not going to let you get away with not paying something to your creditors. In the past, it would have been up to a judge to determine what would be unacceptable. Now, it's written into the law exactly what is considered an abuse.

THE "MEANS" TEST

THE FIRST step is to look at your income. The court assumes that your income is whatever it was in the six months before you filed. It doesn't matter if you just lost your job. Officially, your income will be the average of the previous six months' income. So you double that to get a yearly figure. Then you see where your income stacks up against other people in your state, as reported by the Bureau of the Census (www.census.gov). If your income is less than the median income for a family of your size in your state—no problem. You are not subject to the means test.

But if your income is the same or higher, then it's onto the next step. You must then determine your "monthly disposable income." This is what you have left over every month, after you pay your basic expenses, such as food, rent, utilities, etc. Actually, it's what the government thinks you should have left over. You see, you aren't allowed to use what you actually spend. You're limited to spending allowances as decided by the Internal Revenue Service (www.irs.gov). These are the guidelines used by I.R.S. agents in negotiating payback plans for delinquent taxpayers. They're not exactly generous.

You're also allowed to deduct some other expenses, such as charitable donations, educational expenses for children under eighteen, and payments being made to certain creditors, such as the I.R.S. and the car loan company. There are limits to all those expenses, too numerous to list here.

Once you deduct the allowable expenses from your monthly income, look at the difference. If it's less than $100, there's no presumption of abuse and you need go no further. If it's above $100 but less than $166.67, you then look to see how much of your debt could be paid off if you gave that money to the court each month. So multiply that figure by sixty. If the result would pay less than 25 percent of your debts, there's no presumption of abuse. If it would pay more than 25 percent, there is that presumption. There's also a presumption of abuse if the figure is more than $166.67, no matter what percentage of the debt that could be repaid.

Are you still with me? (And I thought I wouldn't need math if I became a lawyer.) After doing all these calculations, you may decide that a Chapter 7 wouldn't work for you if you have to go into it with a presumption of abuse. Debtors can still file a Chapter 7, but they must then prove there are special circumstances to justify the use of higher expenses or lower income figures.

IF YOU CAN FILE A CHAPTER 13, IS IT RIGHT FOR YOU?

EVEN IF you're eligible for Chapter 7, there are times when a Chapter 13 makes more sense. Here are some questions to ask yourself:

1. Do you have property that you would lose in a Chapter 7? If you want to keep your house and you'd lose it in a Chapter 7, then you'd certainly want to file a 13, if you're able to. That's probably the main reason people get into the wage-earner plan.

2. Have you fallen behind on the mortgage and the lender is threatening to fore-close? If so, Chapter 13 would enable you to catch up with your payments more easily. Filing either bankruptcy will stop the foreclosure cold. But if you were in a Chapter 7, you'd probably only have a few months before the lender started fore-closure proceedings again.

 In a Chapter 13, you could put all those missed payments into the plan and catch up over the life of the plan. You would resume making the regular payments and, as long you kept up both payments, the mortgage company couldn't take your house. You could also do this with a car, rolling the missed payments into the plan and catching up in years, rather than in months.

3. Do you have a lot of debts that wouldn't be discharged anyway? Chapter 13 may be a better choice for you. For example, if you owe student loans, child support, and recent taxes, you could spread out the debt in payments that you can handle. You'd be making one payment instead of several.

 Of course, if your plan does not call for paying 100 percent of your debts, then you'll be stuck with the balances of those debts after your bankruptcy is over, just as in a Chapter 7.

4. Do you have some debts that would be discharged, but that you want to pay? A common situation is that there is a codebtor, say a mother or a spouse, who is not filing bankruptcy. If the debtor files a Chapter 7, the creditor will immediately go after the other party. In a Chapter 13, the debt would be paid within the plan and the other party would be left alone.

5. What does your gut tell you? If you are really torn up over not paying your debts and you truly believe you can fulfill a plan, then go for it. But don't set yourself up for a fall. If you file a Chapter 13 and it's later dismissed because you can't make the payments, you'll be in even worse shape. Take a hard, realistic look at your situation. Don't make a decision based on wishful thinking. For more on what happens after a failed Chapter 13, see chapter seventeen.

CHAPTER EIGHT

THE 2005 LAW

Actor Burt Reynolds had so many debts he had to file a Chapter 11 bankruptcy, the kind that is usually used by corporations. He had lost money through investments in a dinner theater and a chain of restaurants called Po' Folks. When he filed in 1996, Reynolds listed more than $8 million in debts.

But Reynolds was able to hang onto his $2.5 million estate because he lived in Florida, one of the few states that allows debtors to keep their homes, no matter how expensive.

Reynolds later bounced back. His career experienced a boost with his performance in the movie Boogie Nights.

B Y now, you've probably figured out that I'm not a fan of the law that went into effect October 17, 2005. Here are a few more ways the law has made filing bankruptcy more difficult and expensive.

MANDATORY CREDIT COUNSELING

Everyone who files for bankruptcy must first get some credit counseling from a nonprofit agency approved by the court. This can be done over the phone or on the Internet but it must be within the six months before filing. You'll need to file with the court a certification that you did this as well as any plan that the credit counselor recommended. This requirement may be waived for people who are disabled, incapacitated, or on active duty in a war zone. The law also allows people to get the counseling within thirty days *after* filing if they can show they were unable to get it right before and there was some special need to file right away.

This can certainly complicate things. People facing a foreclosure or a wage garnishment don't have time to get counseled. Even before the new law was signed, clients told me they had to wait several weeks to get an appointment with a credit counseling agency. Some of them came to see me while they were waiting and then realized that bankruptcy was a better option.

I don't know about other bankruptcy lawyers, but most of the people I see are way beyond the counseling stage when they walk into my office. Forcing them to jump through another hoop simply adds time, stress, and expense to the process.

After the case is filed, debtors also have to complete a financial planning class approved by the trustee's office. They'll be denied a discharge if they don't. This requirement can be waived if the local trustee's office determines there aren't enough classes available in that area.

MORE PAPERWORK

Debtors must now come up with a great deal more documentation. Besides the credit counseling certificate I just mentioned, you'll have to produce a copy of your latest tax return at least seven days before your hearing. Your case will be dismissed if you don't. And if anybody asks, you'll also have to come up with copies of tax returns for the four tax years before you filed. I say anybody, but I mean what the law calls "a party in interest" such as a creditor.

You have to file an itemized statement, showing how you came up with your monthly income. You also must provide copies of all pay stubs showing money paid to you in the sixty days before filing. Ideally, since so much depends on income, you should come up with pay stubs for the six months before filing to give to your lawyer. That will help in your decision-making. You should also give your lawyer any communication from a creditor within the past ninety days. The law says that you must use the return address on those statements when you file your case.

In Chapter 13 cases, debtors must provide an updated income and expense statement once a year during the life of the plan. They also must have filed tax returns for the past four years or their plan won't be confirmed.

CHANGES IN DOMESTIC RELATIONS DEBTS

THERE IS one good thing in the new law. Now, child support and spousal support debts are given higher priority when unsecured debts are paid, either through a Chapter 13 or by selling property in a Chapter 7. In fact, those debts are now listed first in priority. They used to be way down the list, even behind claims by "certain farmers and fishermen." It does make sense to pay these claims first.

For years, people who owed child support or spousal support couldn't get out of paying by filing bankruptcy. Those debts could not be discharged. Now, any debt that comes of the divorce is nondischargeable. For example, say the wife agrees to pay a jointly-held credit card as part of a property settlement agreement. In the past, she could have simply listed her ex-husband as one of her creditors in a bankruptcy and he could do nothing. Now, her debt to him survives the bankruptcy. She'll be off the hook with MasterCard, but her obligation to pay it back to protect him remains.

LONGER WAIT TO FILE AGAIN

YOU CAN'T file another Chapter 7 until eight years have passed since the last one. In Chapter 13 cases, you can't get a discharge if you have received a discharge in a Chapter 7 case within four years of the filing of the new one. You'd have to wait two years if it was a Chapter 13.

MORE OPPORTUNITIES FOR CREDITORS TO CAUSE TROUBLE

THE LAW has expanded the definition of what debts are presumed to be non-dischargeable. Now, any debt to a single creditor over $500 for luxuries is presumed nondischargeable if incurred within ninety days of the bankruptcy filing. The amount is $570 and the time period is seventy days if it's a cash advance. Loans taken out to pay nonfederal taxes won't be discharged as well. Student loans have been exempt from discharge for years. The new law expands the definition of what is a student loan.

Since creditors now have a greater ability to object, debtors are likely to find themselves fighting off more challenges in court. This gives creditors a powerful stick. They can threaten litigation if the debtors won't agree to reaffirm the debt. The debtors may find themselves forced to settle because they can't afford to defend themselves in court.

ATTORNEY LIABILITY

THE NEW law holds the lawyer responsible if something goes wrong. Say I file a Chapter 7 but later the court determines that my client wasn't eligible. Maybe a judge decides that some expenses we claimed were not reasonable or necessary. Or perhaps my client didn't tell me about a second job so the income was understated. The law says that I have the responsibility to make an inquiry into all the information to make sure it's correct.

If it turns out later that information was wrong, the trustee could come after me. I could be forced to give back my fee, pay a civil fine, and even have to reimburse the trustee's costs in coming after me.

Also, the new law requires attorneys to identify themselves as a "debt relief agency" in all communications with the public. I think this is misleading as well as cumbersome and annoying. But it's now the law.

Right now you might be saying, "Hey, Nora, why should I care about those provisions? They affect my lawyer, not me." Well, they may affect whether you can find a lawyer. It's not just that an attorney might have to give back a fee if he or she loses when a Chapter 7 is challenged. The attorney might also have to pay for that privilege—the fee of the opposing counsel. I can't think of another area of the law where that happens. This can only discourage lawyers from taking bankruptcy cases. The ones who are left will have to charge more in order to have the time to investigate and document every possible angle. Also, the laws of capitalism kick in. Fewer lawyers can charge more to meet the demand.

I have to wonder if that was a motivation behind the new law. Not only are fewer people able to file, those who still can will find there are fewer lawyers available to help them.

WHAT WASN'T COVERED UNDER "BANKRUPTCY REFORM"

WHAT'S INTERESTING is what didn't make it into the law. Some members of Congress had wanted any bill labeled "bankruptcy reform" to include provisions to rein in predatory creditors. Bankruptcy doesn't occur in a vacuum. Many people fall into a credit trap set by the credit card companies. Credit is too easy to get and too expensive. At a time when most interest rates are the lowest in several decades, credit card interest rates remain high, especially for people with poor credit histories.

Many people who have racked up a lot of debt may not understand how it works. One modest proposal would have required credit card companies to show just how long it would take to pay off a credit card balance if only the minimum were paid. Many people would be shocked if they realized how little of a payment goes to the principal. In the end, the law said creditors may tell their customers they can call the Federal Trade Commission for an estimate of how long it would take to pay the balance by making the minimums. Creditors do have to provide a phone number.

Thanks, guys.

A FINAL WORD ON BANKRUPTCY "REFORM"

IN MY opinion, this was a solution in search of a problem. But nobody asked me. Members of Congress did hear from the credit card companies, which for years have been alarmed by the rising number of personal bankruptcies in the United States. Credit card companies have lobbyists. People thinking about filing bankruptcy don't.

There's something awfully mean spirited about this. Times are tough for a lot of people. Big corporations continue to file for bankruptcy protection, resulting in the loss of jobs and pension funds. Also, jobs have been steadily moving overseas in recent years.

A client of mine reached the end of her rope after a conversation with a bill collector from American Express. She'd been out of work for some time despite her efforts to get a new job. She asked the collections agent where he was and found out he was calling from Bangalore, India. So credit card companies hire someone in India to dun the unemployed here. And yet they got the law changed to make it harder for people to get out from under crushing debt. They insisted the deadbeats were gaming the system.

I've handled lots of bankruptcies over the years and I can tell you, that is simply not what I see. Every once in a great while, a client will come along and I'll get a little twinge that perhaps he might be a little too cavalier about his situation. But in the vast majority of cases, people drag themselves into my office, hoping I can suggest anything except bankruptcy. They're not devious; they're mortified.

I was outraged to hear the congressional debate on the subject, with legislators railing about fiscal responsibility. These are the same guys who've run up record federal budget deficits. I also get annoyed when I hear people say that bankruptcy law should be tough because they pay their bills so everyone else should, too. That's like resenting the Memorial Sloan-Kettering Cancer Center because you don't have cancer.

I'm all for personal responsibility. If you incur the debt, you should pay it. But there are times when circumstances beyond one's control make that impossible, such as the loss of a job, a divorce, or huge medical expenses. It seems to me we could have weeded out the people who are abusing the system without punishing those who truly need a fresh start.

CHAPTER NINE

ALTERNATIVES TO BANKRUPTCY

Hollywood madam Heidi Fleiss filed for bankruptcy after serving three years in prison. In her petition, she listed her occupation as unemployed, but noted that she was about to enter the workplace again.

Fleiss put down nearly $300,000 in debts but only $5,200 in assets, just clothing and jewelry.

BANKRUPTCY is not for everyone. It should not be done lightly but only after a realistic look at the alternatives. If you can't dig yourself out in a reasonable amount of time, you should certainly consider it. In your situation, you have a whole bunch of lousy options and bankruptcy might be the least lousy of them. But it might not be. Let's talk about some options that may be better, depending on your situation. But first . . .

STOP YOUR SPENDING

THIS IS good advice no matter which option you choose. You've got to cut up the credit cards right now. Every quarter you stick on plastic turns into dollars in time. You will never EVER get out of this hole if you don't stop digging. The very first thing you have to do is to stop making the situation worse. Make a budget and stick to it. Figure out the bare minimum you need to get by.

We all waste money, in large and small ways. And I don't criticize most people who spend their money in what I consider to be foolish ways. They would probably think I spend my money foolishly. But you're not most people right now. You're someone who needs to get a grip on your finances. Pack your lunch, combine errands to save on gas, and do without. Forgo that soda out of the machine and figure out where the water fountains are instead. Every dime matters right now.

SEPARATE NEEDS AND WANTS

YOU SHOULD approach this logically and unemotionally. Try to identify the difference between your needs and your wants. The needs are obvious—items such as food, clothes, shelter, health care, transportation, utilities, and childcare. There are ways to economize in those areas. Any book or Web site about living frugally will give you lots of ideas.

The wants, you simply eliminate from your budget completely. Most entertainment falls in that category, such as cable television, movies, and going out to eat. If you are committed to avoiding bankruptcy, you're going to have to live on the least money possible.

SUGGESTED READING:

The Complete Tightwad Gazette. Amy Dacyczyn. Villard. 1998.

Living Well On Practically Nothing. Edward H. Romney. Palladin Press. 2001.

Yankee Magazine's Living Well on a Shoestring: 1,501 Ingenious Ways To Spend Less For What You Need and Have More for What You Want. Yankee Magazine. Yankee Books. 2000.

Frugal Families: Making the Most of Your Hard-Earned Money. Jonni McCoy. Bethany House
Publishers. 2001.

BE RUTHLESS

STOP GIVING to charities, including your relatives. That may sound cruel, but you are
in a serious situation and have to limit your expenses to keeping your immediate
family alive.

If that immediate family includes a grown or almost-grown child, consider en-
couraging the child to get a job. Many parents want to maintain a facade that they can
always handle everything and can easily meet every need or want of the family. That's
not true and not necessary.

Financial troubles are a part of life. Here's your chance to provide some real-life
education for your children. In the case of adult children, they shouldn't be living with
you without paying. Not only do you need the money, you're not doing them any fa-
vors by letting them freeload. They need to know what it means to earn their own way
in the world.

Teenagers could pick up some extra money by cutting grass or babysitting. You
wouldn't expect them to pay rent but they could pay for more of their own expenses
to allow you to reduce the amount that you're spending on them. They might feel re-
sentful now—heck, they're teenagers and resent everything you do. But someday, they
might look back with pride that they were able to contribute to the family in a time of
need.

INCREASE YOUR INCOME

OBVIOUSLY, THIS won't work for many people, but consider whether you can work
overtime on a regular basis or even get a second job. Even just one evening a week
could produce some extra money that you could put aside to pay your creditors.
Maybe you have some special talent or ability that you could turn into cash, for example, tutoring students in algebra. (I haven't been able to help my younger son with
his math homework since the fifth grade.)

You could do yard work or babysitting yourself, if you're not competing with your own teenager.

Be sure that every extra dollar is spent on reducing your debt, starting with the creditor with the highest interest rate. Keep up at least minimum payments for the rest. Keep your eye on the big picture.

LIQUIDATE YOUR ASSETS

If you're like most Americans, you have a whole lot of stuff. And it might be stuff that other Americans would pay cold, hard cash for. If you truly want bankruptcy to be a last resort, you might consider your own personal "Chapter 7," without the help of any court. Sell off your assets. Yard sales don't produce very much, except to reduce clutter. This is a good thing, of course, but not financially lucrative. But there are consignment shops, low-cost ads in local newspapers, and eBay. Again, make sure all the money goes toward your debts. Don't use it to buy more stuff.

You might be able to borrow against a whole-life insurance policy. This is not the kind of insurance you get through work, but an investment that can acquire some cash value over the years. You're actually borrowing against yourself. If you died before it was paid back, the loan would be deducted from the insurance proceeds given to your beneficiaries.

I don't suggest you borrow against your 401(k) or other retirement plan. Those are often protected in a bankruptcy anyway, and cashing them out will leave you with an I.R.S. debt and nothing put aside for your future. 401(k) retirement plans are not tax-free, but tax-deferred. That means that you didn't pay tax on income you earned and then deposited in that account for that purpose. But you will have to pay tax on that amount when you withdraw the money. There are also penalties for taking the money out before you reach retirement age.

Those plans are designed to encourage people to save for their retirement. So there are tax incentives to put the money aside and tax penalties for taking it back and spending it for something else. I'm not saying that no one should ever do that, but no one should do that without consulting an expert and knowing the consequences.

DEBT CONSOLIDATION LOAN

IT IS possible that you can get one big loan to pay off all your little loans, at a lower interest rate than you're paying now. Be very careful. Again, when you're in a hole, the first rule is to stop digging. But this is an option that you might explore, especially if you own a home with a fair amount of equity.

You could even consider selling your house to pay off your debts. This is not a time to be sentimental. You have to take a cold, hard look at your options and decide which one makes the most practical sense. There are lots of factors to consider here, such as the tax break for paying mortgage interest and whether you could rent a place for the next several years for the same amount you're now paying on the mortgage.

If you have a lot of equity in your house, it makes sense to consider tapping into it. You're sitting on a pile of cash you could use to get into a more stable financial situation. Again, don't liquidate anything without being sure of the consequences. If you sell your house for a great deal more than you paid for it, you could have to pay a capital gains tax. Consult with an accountant or tax attorney before taking this step to pay your debts.

NEGOTIATING WITH YOUR CREDITORS

IT'S CALLED a "workout"—you get your creditors to agree to take a smaller amount than you actually owe. You write to all your creditors and tell them that you are considering bankruptcy but would really rather avoid that if they would just cooperate. Offer to pay them a lump sum, perhaps fifty cents on the dollar. (You could use the money you made by selling those Wayne Newton records on eBay.) Or you could offer to pay over time with specific amounts, perhaps at a lower interest rate.

I have to tell you though, that this doesn't work very often. Over and over again, I hear clients say, "The credit card companies wouldn't work with me! It's like they'd rather I file bankruptcy!" That just might be true. The credit card companies are big old institutions, not set up to do anything out of the ordinary.

Smaller, independent creditors such as local merchants and doctors are more likely to work with you. But having a successful workout means getting everybody to go along with the program. It makes no sense to pay some cooperative creditors and end up having to file bankruptcy anyway.

CREDIT-COUNSELING PROGRAMS

BE VERY, very careful of these. It sounds great—these nonprofit organizations will negotiate with your creditors for you. All you have to do is make one monthly payment, smaller than all those separate minimums, and you'll eventually be debt-free.

I don't want to disparage an entire industry. I'm sure there are some good programs that help people and get them back on track. But I have no personal knowledge of those. Since I'm a bankruptcy lawyer, I see their failures, and even their victims.

Many of these "nonprofit" programs are paid for by the credit card industry, so they may not have your best interests at heart. Others charge large up-front, nonrefundable fees and fail to deliver anyway. It might not be completely their fault. Unlike in a Chapter 13 bankruptcy, the creditors don't have to accept negotiated amounts and can insist on being paid in full, which will mess up the whole package. So even if you've agreed to pay the counseling program a certain amount and you follow through, your creditors can refuse to accept the plan. You are still obligated to the creditors for the total balances.

Some of those counselors may be outright crooks. I've heard horror stories from clients who found themselves in even worse shape after trying the credit-counseling route. They paid a good chunk of money that somehow never ended up in the bank accounts of the creditors. Their debts mushroomed with late fees, over-limit charges, and interest.

It could be that because of what I do, I never hear about the good guys. So you might want to explore this option for yourself. Just be sure to read the contract carefully and know what your recourse is if they fail to live up to their promises. Ask them for references. If they're as good as they say, they should be able to come up with a couple of names of happy customers.

FIGHT THE DEBT

YOU MIGHT actually have defenses against some of your debts. Perhaps the debt is not yours or the balance shouldn't be as high as you're being billed. Write to the creditor and request clarification. This might not help. The creditors should provide documentation that the amount is correct but often they ignore you instead and keep sending bills.

Eventually, the creditor might file a lawsuit against you. This is a civil matter, not a criminal one. The creditor is asking a judge to determine whether you indeed owe the money. If a lawsuit is filed, you will be served notice of it. The summons will give you the name of the creditor, the amount being sought, and the name and address of the court where the complaint was filed.

If you want to fight this, you'll have to respond. How you do that depends on local court procedures. You might be told to show up in court at a particular time. Or you could be advised that you can file an answer, which is a written response to the demand by the creditor. If you're not sure what you're supposed to do, call the clerk's office.

If the claim against you is large, you'll probably want to hire a lawyer to represent you. (For ten tips on hiring a lawyer, turn to chapter eleven.) At the least you should consult with one to see if you have any defenses that might work. Possible ones include:

1. The creditor has waited too long to file suit. Every state has a "statute of limitations" that sets out the deadline for bringing a lawsuit in various cases.

2. The amount the creditor is claiming is wrong; for example, if you weren't credited with some payments that you made.

3. That you are not responsible for the debt, that the account is not really yours.

4. That the creditor has added to the balance items that may not be allowed by law, such as attorney fees, when your original application form didn't include such a provision.

5. That you were not properly served notice of the lawsuit.

Most debtors don't bother to fight lawsuits, perhaps because they don't understand the system, or they do understand and fear they'll lose. But sometimes this can be worthwhile. Just the fact that you are disputing the suit may prompt the creditor to settle for less than the full amount. Although the creditor was reluctant before to work anything out, it might be more willing once things get to this point.

If there is no resolution, eventually the case will end up in front of a judge. The creditor makes its case and you or your lawyer make yours. The judge decides.

This option will make no sense if you have a lot of debts and not very many defenses. You'd be spending all of your time in court and, probably, you'd be losing. I don't suggest hiring a lawyer to defend lawsuits that you're likely to lose anyway.

Money is scarce right now. You'd be better off spending what little you do have to decrease your debts or to hire a bankruptcy attorney.

DO NOTHING

THIS ISN'T a great option for most people, but I feel duty-bound to mention it. Sometimes in my practice I come across a person who is what we call "judgment proof." This means that even if a court judgment were imposed, the person would have nothing to lose and the creditor would have nothing to gain.

Typically, it's an older or disabled person who is not working. They're living on Social Security or some other kind of government assistance that cannot be attached by creditors. They have no assets, not even a bank account.

Creditors often threaten a lawsuit but don't always follow through. Sometimes the amount isn't large enough to warrant litigation. If the creditor were in another state, it would have to hire a lawyer where the debtor lives. Even if they do sue, they'll quickly discover there is nothing to get and may eventually write the debt off. But this could take years. In the meantime, the debtors may still be getting the dunning letters and the nasty phone calls.

THE FAIR DEBT COLLECTION PRACTICES ACT

HERE'S A good place to mention the Fair Debt Collection Practices Act. This law is designed to prevent abuse when bill collectors are trying to collect a debt.

As I mentioned before, debt collectors are prohibited from threatening to put you in jail or falsely implying that you've committed a crime. They can't threaten you with violence or use obscene or profane language.

They can't lie about who they are or what they intend to do. (For example, they can't claim to be a lawyer or with the government if they're not.) They can't threaten to sue if they don't intend to, or if they are prohibited from doing so under state law. They can't send something in the mail that looks like it's from a court or the government.

Feeling harassed? That's exactly what the Act is designed to prevent. It says that bill collectors may not use the telephone repeatedly "to annoy" a customer. They shouldn't call at odd hours, such as before 8 a.m. or after 9 p.m.

They're not allowed to call you at work if they know that you're not allowed to receive such calls there. You should let them know, in writing, if that's the case.

They're not supposed to contact other people about you, such as a relative or neighbor, more than once. They can make those calls, but only to find out your phone number and where you live and work. They're not supposed to tell them that you owe them money.

They even have to stop calling you if you insist on it. You write them a letter stating that they may no longer contact you. After that, they can only contact you to tell you they won't contact you again (huh?) or to tell you that the creditor intends to take some action, such as a lawsuit.

I know what you're thinking; bill collectors violate these rules all the time. So what do you do? You can't call the fair debt police to haul them away to jail. Remember, this is a civil matter, rather than a criminal one.

You can report any violations to the Federal Trade Commission and to the attorney general in your state. These days, many states have Web sites that can help you understand your rights and take your report. Keep a notepad by the phone so that you can write down the details of any violation. Be as specific as possible.

Such documentation would also be helpful if you decide to sue the creditor for violating the Fair Debt Collection Practices Act. This suit can be brought either in federal or state court. You might want to consult with an attorney to find out which forum is better for you.

If you win your case, you can be awarded any actual damages you had as well as up to $1,000 just for your trouble. Courts may also require the creditor to pay the costs and your attorney's fees.

You should get very familiar with this law if you decide to deal with your financial troubles by selecting the "do nothing" option. At the least, you ought to be able to get them to leave you alone. And in an ideal world, you might pick up some extra cash as well.

Please note that even if the phone calls and letters stop, you still owe the debt and the company can sue if it wants to. Also, your credit report won't be getting any better.

HIT THE LOTTERY

No, I'M kidding! This is not an option. But I'm surprised by the number of seemingly intelligent people who see such games as a possible solution to their problems. They buy lottery tickets regularly with the hope of making it big. They figure, "Someone has to win. Why not me?" I'll tell you why. The odds are stacked incredibly against you.

That's why I hate those human-interest stories when some deserving and poor person wins the jackpot. I think of all those janitors and mothers of six who didn't win. Now, they may be even more likely to part with their hard-earned money on a losing proposition.

But, you say, your mother-in-law seems to win all the time—five dollars here, a free ticket there. Sure, that's how the lottery gets people to keep playing, providing enough little wins to encourage people to think they can win the big one any day now. I'll bet that if you added up all she's spent on tickets, you'd find she lost more than she won.

Yes, picking up a lottery ticket can be a harmless form of recreation. It's fun to fantasize. But you can't afford the fantasy right now. Besides wasting money, you shouldn't engage in magical thinking, the idea that something will come along and take care of all your problems. The only way you're going to be in better financial shape is to take charge yourself and do what needs to be done.

PART THREE

GETTING READY— PREPARATION IS THE KEY

CHAPTER TEN

YOU DON'T HAVE TO HIRE A LAWYER . . . BUT YOU PROBABLY SHOULD

Everyone knows Larry King. He's the host of Larry King Live, *described by CNN as the first worldwide phone-in talk show on television. He interviews newsmakers from every walk of life—presidents, movie stars, the famous, and the infamous.*

Many people don't know that he filed for bankruptcy protection in 1978, after years of struggling with debts that at one point reached $352,000. The same year he filed bankruptcy, he was hired by the Mutual Broadcasting Network to be the host of a new late-night talk show on the radio, which eventually led to his current success.

So, you don't have any money and the legal fees for filing a bankruptcy seem very high. And, after getting nearly halfway through this excellent book, you figure you know a fair amount about bankruptcy and you just might be able to handle it yourself.

You could file your case *pro se*, Latin for "for himself," meaning you'd come up with the paperwork in the proper form, file it at the right courthouse, and show up at the hearing without a lawyer to represent you.

That's not such a great idea. In fact, I'm tempted to type, all in caps, DON'T DO IT, and let it go it that. I could knock off early today, but you deserve a more thorough discussion of this. After all, this is your case and your decision and you have the ultimate responsibility to make it work.

I'm not saying that every bankruptcy case filed *pro se* ends in disaster. Certainly, people do this on their own and the ultimate outcome may be the same as if a lawyer had been involved. Most people shouldn't take that chance. There's an old saying that a lawyer who represents himself has a fool for a client.

There are lots of annoying little details involved in this work. In fact, if you do hire a lawyer, you should to be careful to pick one who handles a lot of bankruptcy cases. (I'll discuss hiring a lawyer more fully in the next chapter.) Filing a bankruptcy is not just a matter of filling out some forms. You are seeking relief from a federal court. You need to follow the law and the proper procedures.

And the bankruptcy law has just been rewritten in a big way. It probably won't be changed drastically again anytime soon, but courts are handing down decisions all the time that change the law in this area. Your state may occasionally adjust its "exemptions," its limits on what property people are allowed to keep safe from their creditors. Also, the "local rules" that are peculiar to your particular court are frequently tweaked.

Another warning: There are people out there who will offer to prepare your petition at a cut rate. They're not lawyers and usually don't claim to be. They don't represent you and won't be there at the hearing. You won't know that they've led you astray until it's too late. In many jurisdictions, authorities are cracking down on these people because what they are doing is practicing law without a license.

If you decide you really do want to go it alone, be prepared to spend a lot of time in this effort. Think of it as a part-time job. Instead of making money, you're saving money. Approach it with the seriousness and professionalism that you'd use for any important job.

I've already advised you to read up on this. If you decide to represent yourself, you need to read more. Some lawyers have Web sites that provide some information. Be wary of any information you get on the Internet. It's hard to judge sometimes where the information is coming from and whether it's accurate. Plan to spend a day or two at the library to look through its section on bankruptcy. Go through all the books and check out the ones that seem most inclusive.

You'll want to stop by a bookstore as well, for books that describe how to file bankruptcy yourself. Some of them include copies of the forms. Forms may also be available at stationery or office supply stores.

Once you have the forms, make copies so you can use one as a first draft. But before you even think of filing, stop by your local bankruptcy court. There may be some other forms required in your particular jurisdiction.

Every court has it own "local rules" that govern how bankruptcy is practiced. These can be very lengthy documents, so don't expect to be handed a copy. But there should be a copy that you would be allowed to read.

While you're there be very, very nice to the clerks. They know everything and they can be very helpful. Of course, they can't give you any legal advice but they might be able to point you in the right direction.

For example, they'll be able to tell you when the creditors' meetings are held in your kind of case. You'll need to take a day off work, preferably before you file, to see for yourself what's involved.

Plan to spend a few hours to get the feel for the process. Again there may be some local quirks that the books can't tell you about.

For example, in my jurisdiction, the debtor must provide a picture identification and proof of the Social Security number before the hearing can take place. Since the trend these days is not to put the SSN on driver's licenses, the debtor has to bring something else to verify it, such as a pay stub or the card itself.

Debtors representing themselves don't know about the requirement. The notice of the hearing they receive in the mail doesn't mention it. Who carries a Social Security card around with them? Most experts on protecting oneself against crime suggest one shouldn't do that. So, the *pro se* debtors are caught flat-footed when asked to produce such proof. Other jurisdictions may have requirements that could trap you as well. Also, if you watch some hearings you'll be prepared for the usual questions.

I suggest that you go on this field trip before you even file your papers. It might help you to fill them out correctly if you know what the trustee is looking for.

When you do file your papers, ask the clerk if you're missing anything. If you've already visited the clerk's office once or twice, the clerk may remember you kindly and feel sorry for you because you're doing this on your own. Turn on the charm! The clerks can make your life easier.

Make sure you notify the court if you move during the course of the bankruptcy. You'll have to file a change of address and send a copy to the trustee. You don't want to miss any notice that might be sent in your case.

But let me make one more pitch that you hire a good lawyer to handle your case.

Let me put it this way: I'm a fairly intelligent person. If I had the right tools and the proper manual, I could probably fix my leaking faucet. But I don't want to risk that I'll mess it up. I'd rather the job be done by someone who has done it a thousand times before. And remember this will hopefully be a once-in-a-lifetime event for you. Make sure it's done right. Call a professional.

CHAPTER ELEVEN

TEN TIPS FOR SELECTING AN ATTORNEY

Boxer Mike Tyson made an estimated $20 million in one fight with Lennox Lewis in 2002. And he lost. But his high earning power apparently was exceeded by his spending power. He reportedly spent $230,000 on pagers and cell phones and $410,000 for a single birthday party, before filing for bankruptcy protection in 2003.

Tyson's debts were so large, he had to file a Chapter 11 case, just like a company. His largest creditor was the Internal Revenue Service, which claimed he owed more than $13 million in back taxes. His attorney blamed a lot of his money problems on former financial advisers.

Once you have decided to file a bankruptcy and you want to hire an attorney to handle it, you face another decision—*which* attorney should you choose? The Yellow Pages are filled with the names of lawyers seeking your business. As in any profession, there's a lot of good and bad out there. And it is important you don't get stuck with the bad. Here are ten tips to help you find the right person.

1. Find an Attorney with a Lot of Experience in This Field

It's not enough just to hire a lawyer. You should select one who does a lot of bankruptcy filings. Bankruptcy is not brain surgery, but it is a very specific area of the law. You don't want a lawyer who just picks up a bankruptcy case now and then. The days of the lawyer who hangs out a shingle and takes any case that walks in the door are largely over. The law has simply become too complicated, and it changes all the time.

No lawyer, no matter how talented or dedicated, can keep up with more than two or three areas at the same time. This is not to say that you can't decide to hire a large firm that has a general practice. But the particular lawyer assigned to your case should be someone who does mostly bankruptcy cases.

I learned this myself very quickly. At first, I was associated with a legal clinic that took all kinds of cases—divorce, wills, traffic, and, yes, bankruptcy. This was good experience for me, because I didn't know what kind of law I wanted to practice. But it also made me very anxious. The legislature kept changing the law. Higher courts kept issuing decisions that changed the way the laws were interpreted. How could any one lawyer keep up with all that? The truth is, she can't.

You only have one bankruptcy to file. You need an attorney who knows more about filing bankruptcies than about drafting wills or suing a dry cleaner. Besides familiarity with the subject matter, your lawyer should be a familiar face in the jurisdiction where your case will be filed. If all goes well, you won't have to see a judge, but your attorney ought to be someone who knows the territory. Local knowledge is important, because some trustees are pickier than others. Your attorney should know what to expect, so that you will be completely prepared.

We are all supposed to be equal under the law, but the law is administered by people. And people have human relationships, not abstract ones. Trustees who see a lawyer often and respect his or her credibility may look less critically at a debtor represented by that lawyer. A lawyer's reputation, for better or for worse, accompanies the client through the process.

2. Ask Friends and Relatives for Recommendations

This may not seem like a very helpful suggestion. If you're like most people, you're embarrassed about your situation and you don't want anyone else to know your business. But you might want to put your pride aside and seek advice from people whose opinions you trust. There are ways to get pointed in the right direction without revealing any details.

For example, maybe you know someone who has just had an experience with the legal system. It can be completely unrelated to bankruptcy, such as getting a divorce or having a will drawn up. Ask if that person was pleased with the lawyer and would use him or her again. You could then call that attorney on your own and ask for a referral to someone who handles bankruptcy. Good lawyers know other good lawyers. They're usually happy to send business their way.

When calling the lawyer, you can always use the old, "I have a friend . . ." bit. But you don't have to. Lawyers are used to hearing far worse stories than the one you have to tell. And, as we discussed in earlier chapters, there is nothing shameful about filing for bankruptcy protection.

3. Check with Bar Referral Services

Many lawyers join the bar associations in the cities or counties where they live and many of those associations operate referral services for the public. Here's how it works: You call them and say, "I need to consult a lawyer about personal bankruptcy." The service will give you the name of someone who practices in this field. You then set up an appointment for a consultation, frequently at a discounted rate.

You are only committed to that one consultation, but you may want to hire that lawyer after the meeting. If not, at least you get a chance to ask all your questions and you get a better feel for how the process works. This is also a good way to get a second opinion. Perhaps you decided on a lawyer but aren't quite sure if the information you've been given is correct. By springing for a one-time consultation, you can set your mind at ease or decide that you need to keep looking for the right lawyer for you.

4. Using the Internet

Many lawyers have been slow to adopt this newfangled technology. But those who have jumped in are worth checking out. You can tell a lot about people from their Web sites. At the least, you'll be able to gauge if bankruptcy is a large part of their practice, or just a sideline.

Do they provide a lot of information, or do they simply direct visitors to call for an appointment? Some lawyers provide an e-mail address. You might be able to get a few questions answered by e-mail, and get a feel for the lawyer's knowledge and responsiveness.

Don't expect free legal advice. This isn't just because they want to get paid, although of course they do. All lawyers have to sell is their time and expertise. But many lawyers are justifiably leery about giving out legal advice to people they don't know. You never know when some voice on the phone or an e-mail correspondent could misunderstand the information. There have been cases where attorneys have been sued for malpractice even when the plaintiff never really became a client.

For this reason, most malpractice insurance companies want their insured to set up a formal framework for representation. There's a definite beginning and a definite end to the attorney–client relationship.

That's why I have a retainer agreement at the beginning of each case and a closing letter at the end. My client and I sign the retainer agreement spelling out my fee, the court costs, and what my representation will cover. After the case is over, I send a letter to close the file formally.

5. Using the Yellow Pages

A lot of lawyers look down on those who advertise their services in mass-market venues such as the Yellow Pages. I don't. I've advertised there for years. I provide a service for a fee, and there is nothing wrong with letting people know that I'm out here. I don't work for a big firm with an illustrious reputation. I can't just hole up in my office and expect clients to find me.

But the Yellow Pages and similar ads are just a start. They're a way for you to find who's out there providing the service you need. You can quickly eliminate anyone who doesn't mention bankruptcy or who lists it as one of twenty "specialties." If it's one of twenty, it *ain't* special. You can tell a lot about a person from the ad he or she places.

For years, I've been advertising in the "guide" section of my local Yellow Pages, where it groups lawyers by practice areas. I have room for one line of copy in my ad, so I say "I understand and I can help." I know, I know, it's incredibly corny. But it communicates my style of working with my clients. It signals that I'm not out to intimidate my clients into trusting me. I've had many people say they decided to call me after seeing my ad *because* they felt they would be able to talk to me more easily.

6. Your Lawyer Must Be Approachable and Willing to Provide Information

This is your case and you need to know everything about it. Look for an attorney who invites your questions. You are an informed consumer. You don't want someone to pat you on the knee and tell you everything will be just fine. In all likelihood everything *will* be just fine. But that is more likely if you understand how the process works and you are completely honest with your lawyer.

7. Hire Someone Who Is on Your Side

This sounds obvious enough. But there are, apparently, lawyers out there who take bankruptcy cases but don't *like* the people who file them. I've had clients tell me they'd first gone to a lawyer who yelled at them for having so much debt! That's completely inappropriate, as well as incomprehensible from a business standpoint.

Bankruptcy is a perfectly legal option. Lawyers who are judgmental on the subject shouldn't be practicing in this area. It could be a sign that they don't handle many bankruptcy cases or they usually represent creditors, rather than debtors.

8. Don't Make Your Decision on Price Alone

I know you don't have much cash lying around. That's why you're filing bankruptcy. But you'll be getting rid of a large amount of debt. This is an investment in your future. If you want the job done right, you'll have to pay the price.

This doesn't mean that the most expensive is always the best. We live in a capitalist system, and lawyers are free to charge whatever they want. But the consumer is also free to say, "No, thank you." Bankruptcy is a fairly competitive area, since people tend to be more price-conscious. So, lawyers who charge far more than everyone else may find that they're not getting much business and lower their fees.

You probably also don't want the cheapest guy in town. Lawyers who charge less than everyone else may be less experienced. Also, they may be able to charge less because they do less. They may not be willing to answer all your questions or attend to all the details that will make your case go smoothly. You're only doing this once. You want it done right.

Some lawyers quote a lower fee but then nickel-and-dime you to death. Make sure you know exactly what is included in any "flat fee" and what might be considered an extra. Of course, this ought to be in writing. It could be in the form of a "retainer agreement," like the one I described earlier, or it could be an "engagement letter." This is a letter from the lawyer to you, shortly after your first meeting, which spells out the terms of your arrangement. You'll be asked to sign a copy of the letter and return it, to show that you've seen it and agree.

I'd be very leery of any lawyer who doesn't routinely put in writing the terms of your relationship, including the likely cost. In fact, the 2005 law requires lawyers to enter into a written contract with their clients.

9. Be Prepared

Before you pick up the phone, pick up a pen (or sit down at your computer). You should make a list of all the questions you want answered. Don't be afraid to walk into the lawyer's office with your list. This is an important decision you're about to make and you need all the facts first. I've prepared a sample checklist below to get you started. It is by no means comprehensive, but it should help you get your own questions down on paper.

10. Listen to Your Gut

Although I put it last, this might be the most important tip of all. Hiring a lawyer is like hiring a doctor. Your choice must be someone that you are both comfortable with and confident in.

You might have found the Johnnie Cochran of bankruptcy law. But if you don't feel right about putting your case in his hands, keep looking.

CHECKLIST FOR MEETING WITH A LAWYER

A. The Attorney's Background
  1. How long have you been practicing law?
  2. How long have you been handling bankruptcy cases in this jurisdiction?
  3. What percentage of your practice is devoted to bankruptcy?
  4. Do you represent creditors as well as debtors? If so, in what proportion?

B. The Cost

    1. What is the usual fee for my kind of case?

    2. If it is a flat fee, what does it include?

    3. If you will bill me by the hour, what is the usual time for my kind of case?

    4. Do you charge extra for phone calls, e-mails, etc.?

    5. Do you have a payment plan, or must I pay in full up front?

C. The Process

    1. How long will it take for you to prepare the paperwork?

    2. Will I be dealing directly with you, or with a paralegal or secretary?

    3. Do you see any potential problems based on what I've told you so far?

    4. Will we have a chance to go over the questions before the hearing?

D. Miscellaneous

    1. What happens if I realize after filing that I've forgotten a creditor?

    2. Will you deal with my creditors before the filing?

    3. Will you handle any reaffirmation agreements with secured creditors?

    4. May I call or e-mail you with any questions I have?

CHAPTER TWELVE

ASSEMBLING THE PAPERWORK

L. Frank Baum, the creator of The Wizard of Oz, *didn't start out as a successful writer. In 1888, he opened a general store, "Baum's Bazaar," in the town of Aberdeen, in the territory that later became South Dakota. The store was badly undercapitalized and didn't attract many customers. It went bankrupt two years later.*

But Baum had started writing down some of the stories he told his children, and he published The Wonderful Wizard of Oz *in 1900.*

Y OUR lawyer will know best how to put your petition together. Still it's up to you to provide all the information he or she will need. Don't be intimidated by the amount of stuff you'll have to come up with—just take it one step at a time.

You've probably done a good bit of the work already in deciding whether you should file bankruptcy in the first place. You've added up your debts and taken a hard look at your income and expenses. All you have to do is put the information together and fill in any gaps there might be.

Your lawyer will most likely have a form for you to complete, similar to the worksheets I provide in the Appendix. If not, you can use those worksheets as a guide. Also, take a look at the example of the actual petition, on page 157, which shows the final result.

YOUR BASIC INFORMATION

AND I do mean basic, such as name, address, and Social Security number. You'll need to list your full name, including any "Junior" or "the III." I wish I had a nickel for every time I got a worksheet back from a client who had written just his middle initial, not full middle name.

Besides your current address, you'll need to put down any other addresses where you've lived in the past two years, including the starting and ending dates. You must file in the jurisdiction where you have lived the most in the previous six months.

Don't worry about having to write down your Social Security number. The bankruptcy courts finally realized the potential for mischief in having that information part of the public record. As of December of 2003, all but the last four digits of Social Security numbers are "X-ed" out for security reasons.

There may be a separate document that you'll sign to verify the complete number, but that paper is not part of the public record. The full number is necessary to make sure that you are who you say you are. At the hearing, you may be asked to show proof of the full number by producing an official document such as the card itself or a pay stub.

YOUR DEBTS

YOU'VE PROBABLY already put them together and maybe even know them a little too well. Now is the time to make sure you have them all. The biggest rule in bankruptcy is to list all your debts and all your assets.

When I say, "list all your debts," I mean everything, even those you intend to pay. For example, you may have decided that you want to keep paying your car note so you can keep the Ford Escort. You might want to pay your dentist so you can continue to go to her. And there are some debts that you will be stuck with anyway, such as student loans and recent taxes. You've got to put them all down.

You might be asked to say whether the creditor is secured or unsecured. A secured creditor is one who is able to take some property back if you don't pay, such as the Escort. The creditor gave you the money to buy the property, so has a security interest in the property until the debt is paid. There is language in the loan agreement that you signed that gave the creditor the right of repossession.

Most major credit cards are unsecured. You may have borrowed money from the creditor to buy some property, but your agreement did not give them a security interest in what you bought. It all comes down to the terms of your credit card application.

Some store cards do claim a security interest in what you bought, such as Circuit City and Best Buy. Don't worry too much about these categories. Your attorney will help you sort this out. The important thing is to list everything.

You should even list potential debts. For example, you might have been in a car accident where you were at fault. No one has sued you yet, but that's a possibility. Make sure you include that among your debts. Estimate the amount of damage that might be involved, or if you have no idea put down "unknown."

Also include any debts that have been claimed against you, even if you think the claims are bogus. Perhaps you had paid the $12.75 to the book club, but you're still receiving dunning notices. Go ahead and list it, but tell your lawyer that you don't think you really owe it. There is a box that can be checked to show you dispute the charge.

For each debt, make sure you include the full address, account number if any, and the amount. Be careful in putting down the address. Many companies have a different address for correspondence than the one used for payments. One company told me that nothing sent to the payment address is even looked at, except for the check.

Put down the most recent amount due, even though that's likely to change, because of interest, late fees, and over-limit charges that will continue to accrue. Don't worry about that. Put down the best information you have. The creditor can't come after you for the difference.

You should also put down when you incurred the debt. Sometimes that's easy, such as in the case of a medical debt or car loan. But a credit card balance is likely to have grown over a long period of time. In that case, put down when you opened the account and when you last charged anything on it. Just the month and year is sufficient, if that's all you know. Do the best you can.

Some lawyers like to have a copy of a recent statement for each account. Others don't want all that paper. If your lawyer doesn't want the statements, keep the stack handy anyway, in case there are any questions.

Make sure your lawyer has a copy of any lawsuit filed against you. He or she will probably have to file papers in the state court to stop that suit. Also, provide the names and addresses of any lawyers or collection agencies trying to collect a debt. You want them to be notified by the court as well as the actual creditor. You want everybody to know that you're filing so they know they have to leave you alone.

YOUR ASSETS

AGAIN, YOUR lawyer will most likely have a form to complete to help you report all your assets. You could also use Worksheet 4 on page 139. In any event, take a look at the actual bankruptcy petition (Schedules A and B) to give you an idea of what the court is looking for.

Actually, the court is looking for almost anything you own. The big things are easy—real estate, a car—but also write down your "stuff" as well, such as household goods and jewelry. You might even want to go through your house or apartment with a clipboard, writing down what you have. Put next to it what you think it's worth. This is not what you paid for it or what you'd have to pay to buy a new one. The value is what you think you would have to pay if you bought another one in the same condition.

If you're having trouble assigning a value to something, you could scan the merchandise section of the classifieds or even drop by a yard sale for comparison purposes. You might be surprised how little your stuff is worth.

The day you file your petition is like a picture being taken—a snapshot showing all your debts and all your assets. So you need to include the "cash on hand," what you might have in your wallet on a given day. You should also put down what you might have in a bank account. Obviously, money goes in the door and then out the door. List an amount that you might typically have in an account to keep it open. These are fluid numbers, of course. But put down your best estimate. You can always update it later.

Speaking of accounts, don't forget your 401(k) or individual retirement accounts. Most of them are protected and can't be touched by the trustee, but the trustee needs to know about them in any case.

All other investments such as stocks, bonds, and whole-life insurance policies must be listed. If you just have life insurance through your job, you probably have a term life insurance policy, which has no cash value. With that kind of policy, no one gets any money until you die. Even the bankruptcy trustee won't make you do that! Whole-life insurance, on the other hand, is an investment. After a time, you can borrow against it or surrender it for a certain amount of money. If you have one of those, contact the company and ask for a statement to show the "cash surrender value." The trustee will most likely want to see it at your hearing anyway. And it's best to know in advance how much it is. Lawyers don't like surprises.

Similarly, you'll want to get documentation on your other assets. Your house, if you have one, is likely to be your biggest asset. If you didn't already figure out what your house is worth as part of the process of considering bankruptcy, now is the time to do it. You don't necessarily have to get a full-blown appraisal but you should at least get a realtor to do a market analysis. Make sure the realtor knows you're looking for an "as is" price, without replacing the carpet or fixing the screen door.

In many jurisdictions, you can find information online about recent home sales in your neighborhood. This can help you come up with a reasonable price for yours.

The Internet is a good way to help you estimate the value of your car. For example, the *Kelley Blue Book* is at www.kbb.com. Another is NADA at nadaguides.com. Both have provided sales information on used cars for years. You can use them free. You look up the make, model, and year; type in the mileage and condition; and out comes a number. Print it out so you can show the lawyer where you got the value.

INCOME

THIS PART is a whole lot more complicated than it used to be. In Chapter 7 cases, it's crucial to whether you can even file. In Chapter 13 cases, it helps determine how much you'll have to pay and for how long. You'll need to be able to show how much money you made in the previous six months. So gather up your pay stubs. If you haven't kept them, perhaps you can get a statement from your employer. You put down your job title, the name and address of your employer, and how long you've worked there.

If your pay varies from paycheck to paycheck—maybe you get overtime on occasion—you should provide at least three pay stubs that cover the range. Obviously you can't count on overtime but you can't completely discount it either. The goal is to give the court the most representative figures possible.

Your job is a bit more difficult if you're self-employed or if your income fluctuates wildly from week to week. You'll still need to come up with some kind of honest estimate of your monthly income. The proof might be a little harder to produce. Be prepared to come up with records for several months, as well as your recent tax returns.

EXPENSES

YOU'VE PROBABLY already done a lot of work on this one, in deciding whether bankruptcy would be an option for you. Still, I'm often surprised how little some people know about what they spend.

A family of five will list $150 as the monthly food budget. *Wait a minute,* I'll say. *You have teenage boys—you probably spend that on milk and cereal!* Besides realistic numbers for food and clothes, you should include a miscellaneous category for expenses you know you have but just can't itemize.

There are many personal necessities that you buy all the time, such as razor blades, deodorant, and panty hose. And there are household staples as well, such as lightbulbs, batteries, and paper towels. Your job is to come up with a lean budget that still provides the basics for your family.

Make sure to put down things that may only come up occasionally, such as car repairs and school expenses. Figure out what you spend in a year and put down one-twelfth of that amount somewhere in your budget. I've included some worksheets in Appendix I to help you get started.

Maybe you need to spend a few weeks keeping track of everything. Write it down every time you open your wallet or your checkbook. Try to think of everything—even things that you don't pay every month. For example, you might pay your renter's insurance only once a year. Figure out one-twelfth of the amount and put it down.

Under transportation, if you own a car, don't forget the cost of maintenance, repairs, tolls, and registration fees. If you don't have a car, you probably have to rent one now and then or pay for a taxi rather than the bus. Or, you might give a friend gas money in exchange for a ride.

Just put down your best estimate. Under the 2005 law, your expenses are limited anyway to standards developed by the Internal Revenue Service. That's right. It doesn't really matter what you actually spend but what the government thinks you ought to be spending for a family of your size in your location. The guidelines can be found at www.irs.gov in the section on individuals. You're allowed to add 5 percent to the food and clothing categories, if you can show that's reasonable and necessary. That's where your receipts will come in. There are also a few other expenses you can include over and above the I.R.S. guidelines. They include assistance to a family member such as a disabled parent and as much as $1,500 per year for educational expenses for children under the age of eighteen.

The budget is important because it helps determine which type of bankruptcy you might file or even if you should file at all. Remember, just because you've hired a lawyer and started the process doesn't mean you can't change your mind. You might decide, after getting into the details, that bankruptcy is not the right option. This is your case and your decision.

CHAPTER THIRTEEN

PRE-BANKRUPTCY DO'S AND DON'TS

Walt Disney didn't just create Mickey Mouse. He started an empire of fantasy, with movies, television, and amusement parks. But an earlier business venture wasn't so successful. As a young man in Kansas City, he decided to join his twin interests, art and photography, with a company he called "Laugh-O-Grams." It went bankrupt a few years later.

So Disney headed west to Hollywood in 1923, where he opened Walt Disney Studios. Many of his full-length animated films won Academy Awards. Disney was also a pioneer in television with the Wonderful World of Color. *Disneyland opened in California in 1955.*

TIMING is crucial in bankruptcy. The day you file, you must list all your debts and all your assets as of that day. But the day you file is up to you and your lawyer. That is one of the many decisions you'll have to make. In this chapter, I'll tell you what goes into making those decisions in the crucial days or weeks leading up to the filing and make suggestions on what to do—and not to do—to make your case go smoothly.

DON'T: MAKE LAST MINUTE CHARGES

LET'S BACK up a bit to the day you decided that you would file for bankruptcy protection. As soon as you think that bankruptcy is in your future, you should immediately stop adding to the debt.

Don't charge anything. In fact, it's a good idea to tear up the credit cards, unless your attorney wants to take care of that. I've had clients tell me they were told by friends or relatives that they could go ahead and "take what's left" of the credit lines of their accounts before they filed bankruptcy.

What does this mean? It turns out they were talking about charging right up to their credit limit and then filing bankruptcy, when they owed an even higher amount. This is wrong. First, it's fraudulent because they know when they're incurring the debt that they have no intention of paying it back.

Even if it weren't morally wrong (which it is), it is legally risky.

Under bankruptcy law, creditors can object to a particular debt being wiped away. The typical reason is fraud. When the creditor gets the notice that you filed, it takes a look at your account history. If it sees a bunch of charges right before filing, it will get suspicious. The creditor can claim that you planned to take money that you had no intention of repaying.

That doesn't mean the creditor will automatically cause trouble. If the amounts were small, the creditor might not bother about it. But you shouldn't give the creditor any reason to be suspicious.

DO: TELL YOUR LAWYER EVERYTHING

YOU DON'T want to be special in bankruptcy. Your goal is have your case slide on through the system, with no red flags and no questions raised. That's why it's important that you tell your lawyer everything about your case.

When I have a client who listened to a wacky friend and made some last-minute charges before coming into my office, I usually advise two things.

First, I suggest that, if at all possible, we wait a few months before filing. Under the law, the burden of proof is on the creditor to show that a particular debt should not be discharged. This means that the debtor doesn't have to prove that he or she didn't intend to defraud anybody. It's up to the creditor to prove that intent. So, how can a creditor get inside the debtor's head and show that the debtor wanted to take the money with no idea of paying it back? Creditors can show a presumption of fraud by the circumstances surrounding the charges.

For example, they can point to amount and the timing. If you charged more than $500 for luxury goods or services to a single creditor within ninety days of filing, it's presumed that you didn't intend to pay it back. The same presumption is made when it's a cash advance of more than $750 within seventy days of filing. The bankruptcy code doesn't spell out what constitutes a luxury, but you don't want to be in a position where that determination is being made by a judge.

Again, the less attention you attract, the better. So in cases where a client has made questionable charges, I suggest we hold off on filing until at least 120 days have passed. The extra time is just a little insurance. Filing on the ninety-first day after a big charge might throw up a red flag of its own. Generally speaking, the more time that passes since the charges, the less likely the creditor will object.

Of course, there are times when you can't wait to file for some reason, for example, to stop a foreclosure or a wage garnishment. But if there is no strong reason to file right away, it's best to wait a bit.

DO: PAY SOMETHING TOWARD RECENT CHARGES

The second suggestion I have for clients who have charged something large recently is that they make some payments to that creditor in the meantime. When the creditor looks at your account, it will look at the recent charges, but it will also look at the recent payments. If you make a large charge right before filing and then make no payments, it will look fraudulent. But if you let some time pass and you make a few payments after the last charges, it looks as if you are indeed trying to pay it back. Think of it as putting an extra quarter in the parking meter. It may not be necessary, but it's a small price to pay to avoid a larger expense down the line.

At the same time, you probably don't want to pay those other guys anything. You can probably safely stop paying on your unsecured credit cards. Except for the situation I described above, you'd be throwing your money down a rat hole. It won't make a whole lot of difference if you manage to send off a $20 minimum payment right before filing. The account will be included in the bankruptcy and it doesn't matter if the total ends up being $2,476 or $2,456.

DO: PAY YOUR BASIC EXPENSES—AND YOUR LAWYER

ALSO, YOU'LL need whatever cash you have for other things. I've seen people let the rent slide so they can send something to that persistent fellow calling from Discover. You have to take care of your family first and that means keeping a roof over your head. Of course, you should continue to pay your regular monthly expenses, such as the rent and utilities. If you are planning to keep a car that's being financed, you should try to stay current with that bill as well.

Besides the necessities, a better use of your money right now is to pay your lawyer. Once you've decided that you're going to file bankruptcy, you'll need some legal help. Ideally, you will actually hire an attorney to handle the case for you. Even if you decide to try to go it alone, at some point you should seek professional guidance. Even if all you do is pay for a one-time consultation, you'll need some cash to do that. You've got to prioritize and put your limited resources where they will do the most good.

DON'T: SHOW A "PREFERENCE" TO ONE CREDITOR

ANOTHER FACTOR in paying creditors right before filing involves something called preference. The court doesn't want you to play favorites and pay a chunk of money to some creditors and not pay the rest. It could reach back before the filing and take the money back from that creditor and then spread it around to everyone. This doesn't happen very often but it's something to consider in the days before filing.

It's assumed that a payment is an improper preference if it's more than $600 and made to a single creditor in the ninety days before filing. It doesn't matter if the payments were made all at one time or more than once during the ninety days. If the total is more than $600 in the time period, the payments could be considered to be a preference.

The time period in question is much longer if the creditor is considered to be an "insider," for example, a close relative. In those cases, you have to tell the court if you paid a total of $600 or more for a whole twelve months before filing. So it's not a good idea to pay back your mom a large amount just before you file bankruptcy. The court could very well take it back. You might be wondering how the court would know if you did that. It will because you have to tell it. You sign your bankruptcy papers under penalty of perjury. The worst thing you can do is lie.

By the way, if you can, you should keep your car payment current during this time. It probably adds up to more than $600 in three months. But since the car loan company is a secured creditor, the court won't take those payments back. It only acts when one unsecured creditor gets a large advantage over others in the same category.

DO: CHOOSE YOUR FILING DATE WISELY

ANOTHER FACTOR that goes into the timing of filing of a bankruptcy concerns your property. As I've said before, the day of the filing is like a picture being taken—it shows all your debts and all your assets as of that day. For example, you probably put down in your paperwork what you might have in a checking account. Obviously, money goes in the account and money flows out of the account. If you can, you might want to choose as your filing day a time when there's not as much money, for example, right after the rent has been paid.

DON'T: HIDE ASSETS

SOME PEOPLE want to go too far with this and actually hide their assets. They'll ask if they should take all the money out of their bank accounts before they file. I ask what they're going to do with it. The answer is usually to stick it under the mattress or give it to their brother to hold for them.

Neither scenario will work. Either way, the money is still their property. They still have to list it on their petition, but under the "cash" heading instead of the "checking account" heading. And if they gave the cash to a brother, they'd also have to mention him as the person in possession of the property.

DO: CAREFULLY CONSIDER HOW YOU WOULD JUSTIFY SELLING ASSETS BEFORE FILING

OTHER PEOPLE want to sell off their property right before filing. This can be appropriate, but you should be careful. It might make sense to liquidate some property that wouldn't be protected under your state laws. You could sell something and then use the money to catch up on your basic expenses and pay your bankruptcy attorney. You could also use the proceeds to pay a debt that wouldn't be discharged anyway, such as recent taxes or child support. In that situation, you'd be doing yourself what a bankruptcy trustee would do anyway.

Let me explain. If you did have property for the trustee to take, he or she would sell it and then use the money to pay your creditors, starting with the priority creditors. In effect, you'd be doing this on your own, selling something that can't be protected and giving the money to a debt that can't be discharged.

You'd still have to tell the court about this: first that you sold something and second that you paid someone. But the court would be unlikely to disturb a transaction that has the same result as if the court had taken care of it. You have to make sure that you can justify the circumstances.

For example, if you sold your car to that helpful brother of yours for ten bucks, the trustee would raise an eyebrow. You can't take less than full value for something to keep the money away from your creditors.

A certain amount of pre-bankruptcy planning is allowed. But I can't say exactly how much would be allowed in your case. Courts have interpreted this in different ways. You'll need to talk to a lawyer in your area to find out what is acceptable in your jurisdiction.

The main rule is to disclose, disclose, disclose. First tell your lawyer everything about your case and get some guidance on what you should do. Then, make sure that everything is listed somewhere on your petition when you file. The most trouble you can get into with a bankruptcy court is by hiding something.

DO: GET CREDIT COUNSELING

IT'S NOW required anyway. So you may as well get it over with. As I mentioned before, there can be a long wait to get an appointment to see a counselor. You don't want to be in the position of being ready to file and unable to do so because you haven't taken care of this. There is a way to file first and then get the counseling. But you'd have to show special circumstances. Again, you don't want to do anything to draw attention to yourself in bankruptcy.

PART FOUR

THE PROCESS

CHAPTER FOURTEEN

THE FILING

Singer and movie star Debbie Reynolds decided to get into the hotel-casino business. She bought a property in Las Vegas in 1992 and renamed it the "Debbie Reynolds Hotel/Casino/Hollywood Movie Museum." It failed five years later. The casino filed a Chapter 11 bankruptcy and Reynolds filed a personal one to protect herself from the financial fallout. The hotel was auctioned off and bought by the World Wrestling Federation.

THIS is a very important day for you. As soon as you file, everything stops. You are now under the protection of the bankruptcy court. Your creditors are no longer allowed to contact you. Any lawsuits against you must be suspended.

READ BEFORE YOU SIGN

YOU WILL be bound by the information in your bankruptcy petition. It is possible to amend the paperwork later on, but it's best to do it right the first time.

Before you can file your bankruptcy petition, you need to sign it. This isn't just dashing out your signature on a dotted line. The petition usually runs at least thirty-five pages and you need to read every one of them. In Chapter 13 cases, you may also have the plan to review and sign. If the plan can't be filed simultaneously with the petition and schedules for some reason, you'll have to come back for that. The plan has to be filed within fifteen days of everything else.

Again, this is your case and your responsibility. You'll be signing the paperwork under penalty of perjury, meaning if you lie or hide something, you could be charged with a federal crime. Later, at your hearing, you may be asked—under oath—if you read your paperwork before you signed it. You want to be able to answer honestly that you did.

This may sound obvious, but never sign forms that are incomplete. It's possible—in fact it's likely—that there were will be some changes or corrections that the lawyer will have to make after you sign. But never sign blank forms. This is good advice in any situation.

So be prepared to spend at least half an hour at the lawyer's office, going over everything. Bring along a copy of the worksheet that you provided to the lawyer, so you can double-check the information.

Don't worry that your lawyer will think you don't trust him or her. Good lawyers are very picky and don't mind if you are, too. They'd probably welcome the fact that you are taking responsibility for your case. Lawyers don't want mistakes, either, because it reflects badly on them. This is your only case but most likely one of many for the lawyer. Attorneys want to have the reputation that their cases are done right the first time. And under the 2005 law, they can be held liable if the information is incorrect.

Being thorough at the signing may also help you remember things that may have been overlooked. For example, actually reading the question about closed financial accounts might prompt you to recall that you had shut down a checking account several months ago. This process gives you one more chance to make sure that your paperwork is complete.

The session also gives you an opportunity to ask any questions that you might have. You may have been a bit overwhelmed by the whole thing the first time you met with the attorney. Now, you may have a better sense of what you don't know and need to ask.

Once you've read everything, made all the corrections that need to be made, and signed all over the place, the paperwork is ready to be filed. In the past few years, many jurisdictions have adopted electronic filing, meaning your lawyer can file over the Internet. This can speed up the filing date. No longer are we limited to business hours. We can file at night, on weekends, even at 2 o'clock in the morning if we want to.

ASK FOR YOUR FILING DATE AND CASE NUMBER

ONCE YOUR case is filed, that automatic stay goes into effect, which means there is a court order that no creditor may try to collect a debt. You may want to ask your lawyer to call you when the case is filed and give you the case number. That way, if a creditor does call you, you can say that they have to leave you alone. Once they get the case number, they'll want to leave you alone anyway.

You need to be aware of the filing date for another reason. It's the cutoff date for listing all your debts. So if you incur a debt the day after filing, it's not included in your bankruptcy. Part of being responsible for your own case means knowing the important details.

If you realize after you filed that you forgot something, let your lawyer know right away. You can amend the schedules and even add a creditor after the case has been filed. You want everything to be accurate. And you have a continuing obligation to the court to make sure that your information is up-to-date.

CHAPTER FIFTEEN

THE HEARING

Probably not too many people know that Henry Ford had two car companies that failed before he started the Ford Motor Company. It's true. The first company went bankrupt and the second was dissolved after he had a falling out with a business partner.

But there is no question that the Ford Motor Company proved Mr. Ford could indeed make some money in the car business.

OKAY, the day you've been dreading is approaching. I know this probably won't help but don't panic. It's most likely not going to be as bad as you imagine. (Reality is never as awful as what you can conjure up with a vivid imagination.)

It is important that you be prepared. If you didn't discuss the hearing with your lawyer when you signed your papers, now is the time to bring that up. I can tell you generally what to expect, but this is one of those areas in which local knowledge is important.

For example, in some areas, the trustee will want to see a copy of the title to your car or the deed to your house. Others simply accept whatever numbers you put down in your paperwork. Not only can this vary from state to state or even different jurisdictions within the same state, there are sometimes differences among the trustees. A lawyer who does a lot of bankruptcy in your particular area will know what to expect.

Although your hearing is called a "creditors' meeting," most creditors don't bother to show up. This is not a situation where Capital One, American Express, and Fingerhut will gang up to yell at you. I'm willing to bet that in the vast majority of cases, no creditors will be present at all.

Sometimes, creditors will show up because they think they have to appear. This happens in the cases of private individuals rather than companies, for example a landlord or an ex-wife. They get this notice from the court and they think they have to be present. Sometimes, they think they're going to be paid.

But the only thing that a creditor can do at such hearings is to ask the debtor for information on their debts and assets. Since the automatic stay went into effect on the date of filing, this is their only chance to question the debtor.

Their ability to ask some questions will be limited. For example, they can't ask, "Why won't you pay me?" or otherwise yell at the debtor. The trustees will most likely keep things in line and, of course, your lawyer can object if a question is inappropriate. If a creditor does show up at your hearing, all you can do is answer the questions honestly.

Here's some good advice for anytime you are testifying in a court proceeding. Answer the question asked, only the question, and in as few words as possible. Yes or no answers are the best. Never volunteer any information. Now is not the time to expound on your theories of life. The most important guidance I can give follows what your mother told you many years ago, that honesty is the best policy.

You probably won't have to worry about any creditor. Your main concern will be the trustee who was appointed to handle your case. He or she will have some questions for you, based on the paperwork you already filed.

THE CHAPTER 7 HEARING

IN CHAPTER 7 cases, the emphasis will be on the property you own. For example, you'll be asked if you own any real estate. Many trustees will want to see a copy of the deed and a recent payoff statement from your mortgage company. Some even want to see the "HUD-4," the statement that outlines the details of what happened when you bought the house.

Similarly, some trustees will want to see the title to any car that you own and payoff statements from any car loan companies. You might be asked if you have any life insurance of cash surrender value or if you are now owed a tax refund from any government. If you do have an interest in a whole-life insurance policy, you might want to bring along a copy of a statement, showing the current value if you cashed it in.

You'll also want to be prepared to show how you arrived at your income figures. You should already have filed a tax return and some pay stubs. You might want to bring everything that shows your income for the past six months. Your lawyer probably already has this stuff in your file, but it doesn't hurt to be doubly ready for any question that might come up.

THE CHAPTER 13 HEARING

IN CHAPTER 13 cases, it's likely that even more emphasis will be placed on your income. The whole idea is to see if the plan you've proposed is reasonable, to verify that you do have the income to make your Chapter 13 work. As in Chapter 7 cases, you should already have filed a tax return and some income statements. In Chapter 13, you might want to bring any pay stub you might have received since the filing.

YOUR OBLIGATIONS TO THE COURT

IN BOTH kinds of cases, the trustee will most likely want to know if you read your papers before you signed them and whether you listed all your debts and all your assets. Maybe you realized after the filing that you missed something. Notify your lawyer right away, preferably before the hearing. That way, when you get to that question about listing everything, your lawyer can whip out a copy of the amendment that's been filed to correct the oversight.

In bankruptcy, you are under a continuing obligation to tell the court everything. It doesn't end with the filing. If you suddenly realize that you left something out, you should call your lawyer as soon as possible and arrange to correct the record.

In both kinds of bankruptcy, you'll be asked to confirm that you are who you say you are. Some trustees will ask for a daytime phone number or both home and work telephone numbers. You'll probably have to produce some kind of identification that has your picture on it as well as something with your Social Security number. The court is concerned about identity theft and the possibility that someone will file bankruptcy under someone else's name.

It used to be that many states used the Social Security number on driver's licenses so just one form of ID would work for both purposes. But the trend these days is against using Social Security numbers in that way, to avoid identity theft. If you can't find your Social Security card, you'll need to come up with something else, such as a pay stub or a health insurance card. Talk to your lawyer in advance to find out what is considered acceptable in your area.

PRACTICAL CONSIDERATIONS

SHOW UP at the designated place at the right time (a little early, please) and wait for your case to be called. In many jurisdictions, the hearings are not held in a courtroom but in an ordinary office building. Depending on the caseload in your area, there could be ten, fifteen, or even more cases scheduled for the same hour.

Please dress appropriately. You don't have to dress up as if you're going to the White House, but don't dress for the beach either. And certainly don't go out and buy an expensive new outfit. Perhaps you should dress the way you normally dress for work (unless you're a lifeguard, of course). Be respectful. This is a legal process.

Unless you're first on the docket, you'll probably be able to watch some hearings before it's your turn, so you'll be able to see how it goes. If anything is said that you don't understand, you'll have a chance to ask your lawyer about it. The other side of that is everybody will be able to watch your hearing. Yes, this is usually an open process.

People get upset when they realize that there will be an audience. They're embarrassed to be there and don't want any witnesses to their shame. They're terrified that they're going to run into someone they know.

I often tell my clients this story from my childhood. I was the third of three girls growing up, so I usually wore hand-me-downs. The two exceptions every year were for Easter and back to school. So my mother would take me to a place that I remember as "Miracle Mart."

It could be another name—it's been a long time—but it was a discount store. I didn't mind when I was little, but as I approached my teen years, I was mortified. What if anyone saw me buying my dress at Miracle Mart? Then I realized that if anyone I knew was in the dress department at Miracle Mart the week before Easter or a few days before school started, she would be there doing the same thing.

So don't be worried about seeing people you know at your bankruptcy hearing. Unless they're bankruptcy lawyers or creditors, they're there for the same reason you are. And repeat after me, "Filing bankruptcy does not make me a bad person."

In the majority of cases, the hearing goes well and there's no problem. In fact, it can seem anticlimactic. That's a good thing. In most Chapter 7 cases, this hearing will be the debtor's only appearance. You walk out the door and you're free.

Chapter 13 cases can be a little more complicated, mainly because they go on for so long. Some jurisdictions require the debtor to appear at a separate hearing to confirm the plan. Again it should be a routine matter. Your lawyer should know in advance if there's any problem with your case.

The key is to be prepared. Make sure you find out from your lawyer exactly what to expect and what you need to bring with you.

And try not to panic.

CHAPTER SIXTEEN

TYING UP THE LOOSE ENDS

Country singer Tammy Wynette hit it big with her 1968 single "Stand by Your Man." It was just one of seventeen number-one country hits for her in the 1960s and 1970s. But her fame didn't keep her out of bankruptcy court. Wynette filed in 1988.

IF all goes well, there won't be a whole lot to do after your creditors' meeting. If you're doing a Chapter 13, you may have to attend a hearing to confirm your plan. And of course, you'll have to keep up your payments. Many Chapter 13 bankruptcies fail because the debtors just couldn't do what they had hoped they could.

In Chapter 7 cases, your creditors' meeting may be the last of your obligations to the court. Make sure you ask your lawyer while you're there if there is anything else you need to do in your case.

DEALING WITH SECURED CREDITORS

A COMMON task is to deal with property that secures a debt, for example, a car. When you signed your petition, you should have signed something called a "Statement of Intention" that said what you intended to do with property that secures a debt.

Secured creditors are entitled to their money or their property. You have three ways you can deal with this. Let's look at each option.

REAFFIRMING THE DEBT

PEOPLE OFTEN want to keep their cars despite the bankruptcy. Signing a reaffirmation agreement is one way to do this. Your lawyer probably wrote to the car loan company right after you filed to let it know if you wanted to do this. Either your attorney or the attorneys for the loan company would write up a reaffirmation agreement for everyone to sign.

The agreement would legally obligate you to the loan, as if the bankruptcy never happened. You and a representative of the loan company would both sign it to show you agree with the terms of the contract. Your lawyer would also sign, to certify that you are signing it freely and voluntarily and that paying back that debt would not be a hardship to you or your family.

Usually, the agreement follows the same terms as the original contract—the same interest rate and monthly payments. Once in a great while, a car loan company will agree to make the terms more favorable, for example to lower the balance or the interest rate. If the debtor says "this is not worth anywhere near what the loan balance is, so maybe I should just give it back," the lender may be willing to deal. It really doesn't want your car. It wants your money.

REDEMPTION

ANOTHER WAY to keep the car is called "redemption," meaning you are buying the property back from the creditor. You would have to come up with the money in one lump payment. You may receive some ads in the mail from car loan companies offering to help you with this option. Be careful. Some want to loan you the money at an exorbitant interest rate that could end up costing you more than you are paying your original loan company.

There are some legitimate companies out there. I can't give any specific recommendations since I can't predict whether a good company will go bad by the time you're looking into this option. Do the research and talk to your lawyer. If you do decide to try to redeem your car rather than reaffirm the entire debt, there's a special procedure you'll have to follow.

SURRENDER THE CAR

I FREQUENTLY recommend that a client simply surrender the vehicle. The whole point of bankruptcy is to get a fresh start. It doesn't make much sense to start out encumbered by old debt. Usually these car loans are "upside down," meaning the vehicle is worth less than the outstanding balance. Often they're way, way upside down. People with long-term credit problems are likely to pay a much higher interest rate than most people. The time period of the loan may also be longer than for people with good credit.

Sometimes old car loans are rolled into new car loans, making the balance even more ridiculous. Any financial expert will say that that is not a good idea. You end up paying off two cars at the same time. But people don't always see the financial implications of their decisions. They're looking at the monthly payment, not the whole picture. Or they're just blinded by the prospect of getting a nice shiny new car.

It can happen that people feel forced to get another vehicle this way. They suddenly find they have to buy something else, and can't afford to pay off the old loan as well.

I once had a client who traded in a van for a truck that left him with a huge debt. This was in the fall of 2002, during the sniper attacks in the Washington, D.C. area.

Early eyewitnesses said they saw a white truck at the scene of shootings. So everybody was on the lookout for a white truck. There was even a reward offered for anyone who had information that would lead to an arrest and conviction. As it turns out, a white truck wasn't involved. The men convicted of some of the shootings drove a blue Chevrolet Caprice. But at the time, white trucks were constantly being pulled over.

My poor client had a white van that must have looked like a truck to nervous citizens. He kept getting stopped and questioned by the police. After this happened several times (he was even put in handcuffs), he decided he had to get rid of the van at any cost. He bought another kind of vehicle in a different color, rolling the first loan into the second. He stopped attracting the attention of the police, but he ended up owing a great deal of money.

This was one factor in sending him off the financial cliff and into bankruptcy a few years later. He was able to give back the truck and not owe anything. It just didn't make any financial sense to pay off a vehicle at such a high cost.

Of course many people are reluctant to give the vehicle back. They always say "but I need my car to get to work!" That may be true, or it could be they haven't tried to imagine life without their own automobile. Some areas have good public transportation and some don't. It may be possible to move closer to work. Getting another place to live may end up being more cost-effective than paying off a car loan.

It could be possible to put aside the car note money for awhile and buy a junker outright. It won't be pretty. It might break down more often, but it might get you where you need to go until you can afford something better.

It is possible to get a car loan after a bankruptcy. It has to be completely over. Car loan companies will want to see a copy of your discharge order. You will certainly pay a higher interest rate than people who haven't gone through a bankruptcy. And it's a good idea to have a large down payment. But if you're not making car payments, you might be able to get the money together.

If you decide to give back your car and owe nothing, you may not have to surrender it right away. Once you file the bankruptcy, you can't give the car back without the permission of the court. Even though it's clear the trustee won't want to take the car, you've got to wait until he or she officially abandons any interest in it.

When you filed, you received an order from the court warning you not to dispose of any of your property. Everything came under the jurisdiction of the court. In a Chapter 7 bankruptcy, it's up to the trustee to decide if you have anything that can be sold to pay your creditors. If the trustee took your car, he or she would have to pay the car loan people first. Obviously, that won't work if the car note is more than the value of the car.

When a client decides to surrender his car, I usually write to the car loan people and explain that to them. I also remind them that I can't allow my client to give it back just yet but must wait for the permission of the trustee. I tell them to call me after the hearing and I'll arrange for the return of the vehicle. In the same letter, I also ask for a copy of the title to show that they are indeed secured.

CARS: OTHER POSSIBILITIES

DON'T LET yourself get too excited, but listen to this: Once in a very great while, the people who hold the car note haven't done their job and the loan isn't really secured by the car. A loan secured by a vehicle must be "perfected," meaning the title registered with the state must reflect that there is a lien on the property. The lien works as a hold on the property. If the property is sold, the lien must be paid out of the proceeds. If the title comes back showing no liens, then the loan company is in no better position than any other creditor.

This is a rare occurrence. I've seen it only three times in my practice in nineteen years. But in those times, my clients were able to keep their cars without paying for them. In all cases, the cars weren't worth enough for the trustee to want them. Other debtors might end up losing the car to the trustee, but they may be entitled to keep some of the proceeds of the sale, which would allow them to buy something else.

Even if the creditor is entitled to get the car back from you, it doesn't happen right away. I'm amazed sometimes by how long it can take after the hearing for the creditor to get in touch with me to say, "Hey, we want the car back!" Sometimes months will pass. So my client has the use of the car without paying on it. I always advise them to make sure they keep their insurance up-to-date in case something happens in the meantime. You can't count on your lender being patient, of course, so be prepared to give it back when asked.

Sometimes a car loan company will seek the permission of the court to let it re-possess the car, rather than just deal with the trustee and me. When you filed your case, the automatic stay prevented creditors from taking any actions against you. Lawyers for the car loan company will then file a motion with the court asking that the stay be lifted for them. They'd then be allowed to repossess the car.

It seems a little silly to me to go through all that because it can take a few months to get into court. But the lawyers for the creditor are just being careful. They're mak-ing sure that they have the permission of the court before making any move to get the vehicle back.

This can be startling to the debtor who suddenly receives all this legal paperwork, including a notice of a court hearing. People get scared and think they're in trouble or that they'll have to pay back the money. I try to call my clients right away when I get one of these to assure them it's just a routine procedure. I also write back to the lawyers and offer to sign a consent order in advance. There's no point in me filing an answer or showing up in court when my client wants to give back the car anyway.

BUT YOU HAVE TO DO SOMETHING

IN THE past, you could keep the car without either reaffirming or redeeming. You'd simply keep making the payments. As long as you were current, the loan company couldn't repossess. But the 2005 law requires you to either sign a reaffirmation agreement or redeem the car within thirty days of your hearing. If you don't within forty-five days of the hearing, the creditor is then allowed to repossess the vehicle.

HOUSES—REAFFIRMATION

A HOUSE presents a similar situation. If you decide you want to reaffirm your mortgage, you'll want to sign an agreement that will then be submitted to the court. Like other such agreements, it will have to be signed by everyone—you, them, your lawyer—and filed before your discharge order is entered.

Often, for various reasons, no reaffirmation agreement will be filed in time. In that case, you are okay as long as you keep making payments. They can't take back the house unless you fall behind.

SURRENDERING A LEASE

IF YOU decided to get out of an expensive apartment lease as part of a Chapter 7 bankruptcy, you should make plans to move as soon as possible. Your landlord can't evict you during the three months between filing and discharge, unless he already had an order for eviction before you filed bankruptcy. But even if you manage to stay, you may be liable for the rent after the filing and until you move.

CREDITORS WHO CLAIM A SECURITY INTEREST

SOMETIMES A creditor will pop up and claim a security interest in some other property. For example, I'll get a letter from Circuit City wanting to know what my client intends to do about something she bought there. It may helpfully include a reaffirmation agreement for my client to sign.

If the creditor is truly secured, it is entitled to its money or its property. However, I need proof that the creditor has that status. I printed up some labels that say, "Please send proof of security interest and a description of the property," which I slap on the Circuit City letter and mail back.

Many times, I don't hear from them and that's the end of that. But it's possible that they could cause some trouble later on. Although the debt was discharged in bankruptcy, they could sue you in state court for the return of the merchandise. That's not likely, but it could happen.

Here's how I deal with this kind of situation. If I do receive proof of the security interest and a description of the property, I call my client and ask how attached she is to that flat screen TV.

I never suggest that anyone sign a reaffirmation agreement for this kind of thing. The property is never worth as much as the amount of the debt. But sometimes it's worth something to my client so I negotiate with Circuit City. Actually the negotiations are fairly one-sided. I ask my client what she's willing to pay for it—$50, $100? So I offer that amount. Usually, the creditor will take it. They really don't want your used TV. And $50 is better than nothing.

Sometimes, the merchandise is gone. It broke and was thrown away or was lost in an eviction. In that case, I write to the creditor and explain that she would love to surrender the property, but she can't. I usually end the letter with "I'm sorry I can't be more helpful." That's usually the end of that.

The creditors rarely pursue these matters because it would usually cost more time and money than the property is worth. Some lawyers figure their clients can simply ignore these creditors because most likely nothing will happen anyway. That's probably true, but I think it's better to tie up any loose ends if possible. I don't think it's a bad thing for my clients to pay something for property that is secured. After all, they're getting rid of most other debts. They can always give it back if they feel they can't afford to pay.

LENDERS WITH LIENS ON PROPERTY

THERE'S ANOTHER creditor that sometimes tries to assert a security interest, but on shakier grounds. One of my ten signs that one may be headed for bankruptcy is desperate borrowing. There are some lenders who target people with less-than-perfect credit. They charge high interest and sometimes require the borrower to promise their belongings as collateral.

The agreement might actually list things such as "17-inch Sony TV, 50 compact discs, vacuum cleaner." These creditors are not in as good a position as Circuit City or Dell Computer. Circuit City or Dell probably have a "purchase money security interest," meaning the money that was borrowed was used to buy the stuff. But the secondary lenders are trying to claim an interest in property that was bought long before the debt was incurred. They can make a tenuous claim, but it's going to be hard for them to prove that they should be able to repossess anything.

There is a procedure by which you can go into bankruptcy court and get a judge to void the lien. That may be worth doing or it may not be necessary, depending on the tenacity of the creditor. Most of these guys end up leaving you alone. They really don't want your stuff.

COPING WITH WINDFALLS AFTER BANKRUPTCY

ANOTHER LOOSE end that might come up in Chapter 7 cases is if you suddenly come into some money. You have to tell the court if you inherit money, receive some as the result of a divorce settlement, or are the beneficiary of a life insurance or death benefit plan. This requirement continues until 180 days after your case is filed, meaning you could have to make such a declaration after your case has been closed. The court could revoke your discharge if it finds out you received money under these circumstances and didn't let it know.

MAKING ADJUSTMENTS TO YOUR CHAPTER 13 PLANS

IN CHAPTER 13 cases, you may have loose ends periodically throughout the plan. For example, you might suffer some income loss that makes it impossible to meet your payments. You might be able to rework the terms of your plan to lower your payment—by extending the time period or decreasing the percentage that will go to the unsecured creditors. The trustee might allow you to skip a payment or two and make it up later if it appears to be a temporary problem. But don't head back into the land of denial. You've got to deal with any complications right away.

Suppose you land a job that pays much better? You could pay extra into the plan to give you some cushion in the future or even to pay off your plan earlier. Some trustees monitor debtors to find out if there's any significant increase in income and then insist you modify your plan. Of course, if that happens, you have to comply. But if it's up to you, it's probably better not to change the plan officially but to voluntarily pay extra. That way, you're not locked into a higher amount that you might not be able to afford if the new job doesn't last.

Also in Chapter 13 cases, you might have to head back to court to sell property under the control of the court or to incur new debt, for example, to buy another car when your old one has worn out. Whether you can do that will involve the same kind of analysis used when you first decided on a Chapter 13 and began fashioning a plan.

Under either form of bankruptcy, you have to keep the court informed of your address as long as you're in bankruptcy. (Chapter 7 cases are usually closed about three months after you file.) So if you move, let your lawyer know and he or she will file the new address with the court, with copies to the trustee. If something comes up in your case and no one can find you, there could be trouble.

CHAPTER SEVENTEEN

CONFRONTING THE THINGS THAT CAN GO WRONG

Ulysses S. Grant was first a military hero, then a president. He commanded the Union troops during the Civil War and was elected to the nation's highest office in 1868. But after leaving the White House, Grant became a partner in a financial firm that went bankrupt.

Grant began writing his memoirs as a way to pay off his debts and take care of his family. He died in 1885, shortly after he wrote the last page.

PROBABLY the biggest problem that can arise in either kind of bankruptcy is for someone to object to something. The fallout is different depending on the kind of bankruptcy and who is doing the objecting.

RESPONDING TO THE ACCUSATION OF FRAUD

FOR EXAMPLE, in Chapter 7 cases, a creditor might object, claiming that a particular debt should not be discharged. The usual reason is fraud, as I discussed in chapter thirteen—Pre-bankruptcy Do's and Don'ts.

It's not easy to prove fraud. That's a good thing from my perspective. The only time a court should disallow a claim is when it's clear that the debtor has intended to defraud the creditor.

It always amuses me when I get some correspondence from a lawyer for a creditor suggesting that he might object to a debt because at the time the debt was incurred, the debtor didn't have enough money to pay for the transaction.

Well, gee. Someone uses a credit card because she doesn't have enough cash in her wallet. That's fraud? I thought that's what credit card companies wanted people to do. Under that theory, only people who don't need credit cards ought to be able to use them. It makes no sense to me.

Often, a lawyer for a creditor will send me a letter saying that he is considering filing an objection based on fraud. He'll write, sometimes pompously, that the debtor made charges at a time when he already owed a lot of money to other creditors, and so clearly didn't intend to pay it back. This lawyer either doesn't understand debtors or wants to pretend that he doesn't.

Maybe my practice is an exception, but I rarely see anyone who has plotted and planned to file a bankruptcy. Most are mortified to be there and resisted it for many years.

That resistance can actually make a debtor look worse. Anyone who understands credit card debt knows that the interest rates are outrageous, especially for people with bad credit. Under the terms of the credit card agreement, the credit card company can do anything it wants. It jacks up the interest rate the moment the debtor falls behind in making the payments. It imposes late fees and over-limit fees. It's very easy to double a credit card balance without being able to show anything for it.

Anyone who understands debtors knows that they rarely plan to end up in bankruptcy. They truly believe that they'll be able to catch up some day. They just need a little extra overtime or to hit the lottery and they'll be able to pay off their debts.

I know they're being delusional. But they are making decisions from emotion, not from anything rational. They don't want to file bankruptcy. Sometimes they have to be dragged kicking and screaming to that decision. I rarely see anybody who has decided to file bankruptcy too soon. I have often seen people who decided to file too late. They finally get to my office after they've lost the house or the car or cashed in their 401(k) retirement account.

But no one I see cavalierly incurs more debt with the idea that they won't pay it back. They may be guilty of bad judgment in the way they handle their financial affairs, but they're not guilty of any intent to defraud.

That doesn't stop some creditors from trying. Some of the letters such as the ones I describe above don't seem serious to me. They almost seem like they're trying to shake loose some cash from people who don't know better.

I always respond. I write the strongest letter I can that there is no fraud. I'm as specific as I can be, listing any payments made right before the bankruptcy filing and the reason my clients made whatever charges they did.

I'll mention if my client attempted consumer credit counseling before resorting to bankruptcy. For example, once I got one of these letters from MBNA. The charges in question were made long before the ninety-day period that bankruptcy law views as suspicious. In fact, my client had gone to a consumer credit counseling agency months after the last charges and months before she filed.

I wrote that the consumer credit counseling agency had attempted to negotiate with all her creditors, including MBNA, and never received a response. She obviously had made a good-faith effort to pay off her debts. MBNA didn't want to cooperate then and shouldn't complain now.

I never heard from MBNA on that client again and the discharge order went through without any objection.

DEALING WITH CREDITORS WHO FILE OBJECTIONS

OCCASIONALLY, CREDITORS don't give up that easily. Under bankruptcy law, creditors may not contact the debtor after the filing of the bankruptcy petition. But they can show up at the creditors' meeting and they can request the right to question the debtor at a separate proceeding. It's called a "2004" for the section of the bankruptcy rules that cover that right. The creditor can insist that the debtor submit to a deposition—a proceeding in which the debtor must appear and answer questions under oath.

In a Chapter 7 bankruptcy, creditors have a specific date by which they have to file any objections. It's typically about ninety days after the filing of the petition, and right before the discharge order is entered.

Creditors can ask for more time to decide. They can, right up to the last minute, ask the court for an extension to give them more time to decide whether they will file an objection. Those requests for extensions are routinely granted.

Such creditors should have a pretty good case. First, the creditor must pay a fee to the court in order to register an objection. Also, the creditor will be paying big bucks to its lawyers to pursue any objection. I suspect that lawyers for creditors make a lot more money in bankruptcy court than lawyers for debtors.

A creditor usually files an objection only when it has a pretty strong case of fraud and it involves a fair amount of money. It wouldn't be worth it to go to the trouble of objecting unless the creditor is sure it will win and there's enough money to make it worthwhile.

Even if the creditor has a strong case, it isn't the end of the world. Creditors just want to get paid. Your lawyer could work out something with the creditor for you to pay part of the disputed debt. If the creditor really could win, that's a good resolution. It's worth it to pay them a little bit to avoid protracted litigation that you might lose. That's a judgment call. Your lawyer can give you an idea of whether any claim against you might hold up in court.

If someone files an objection, it doesn't hold up the rest of your Chapter 7 case. You can still get your discharge, as far as the rest of your debts are concerned. But your case won't be completely over until the objection is resolved. Typically, these things get settled. The creditor agrees to drop the objection if the debtor agrees to pay something.

But if the two sides can't agree on a settlement, they end up in court. It's up to the creditor to show why the debt shouldn't be discharged, rather than the debtor to show why it should. And it's up to the judge to decide. The losing side can appeal to a higher court.

INABILITY TO MAKE THE PAYMENTS IN A CHAPTER 13

In Chapter 13 cases, probably the most common thing to go wrong is that the debtor can't keep up with the payments. Many, many Chapter 13 cases fail for this reason.

That's why it's important to make sure your plan is reasonable in the first place. It does no one any good to start this process and then have to abandon it.

Debtors can have their Chapter 13 dismissed voluntarily. There's no hearing involved, but a motion must be filed with the court. The motion is automatically granted unless the case had started out as a different kind of bankruptcy and was then converted to a Chapter 13. In that situation, the court may not let the case be dismissed but insist that it be converted to a Chapter 7.

The debtors, of course, can convert it to a Chapter 7 themselves. Many people really want to pay their debts and try a Chapter 13 when they shouldn't. They have unrealistic expectations of what they can do. So they file a Chapter 13, but then convert it to a Chapter 7 when they realize the truth.

In a Chapter 13, creditors can also claim that you really should be in a Chapter 7, that they would do better if you simply liquidated your assets, rather than tried to pay them off over time. That's one of the tests in a Chapter 13 bankruptcy—whether the creditors would be paid more than if you sold your property in a Chapter 7.

POSSIBLE OBJECTIONS TO YOUR CHAPTER 13

CREDITORS CAN also object to the plan that you proposed to pay off your debts. They could claim that you really should be coming up with more money toward the plan, so that they could get more.

Creditors can claim that you filed your Chapter 13 in bad faith, that you really weren't intending to reorganize and pay your debts, but you had some other motive.

Sometimes people will file a Chapter 13 just to take advantage of the automatic stay. For example, they fell behind on their mortgage payments and they're about to lose their house. But the day before the foreclosure sale (or even on the same day!) they file a bankruptcy. They have no intention of actually following through with a three-year plan; they just want to buy themselves some time.

The filing automatically puts the foreclosure on hold. Even if the Chapter 13 is later dismissed, the mortgage company has to start the process all over again. Some people become serial filers, which suggests they are abusing the system.

Creditors might also raise a "feasibility" objection, claiming that you lack the income to make the plan work. They'd rather you be forced into a Chapter 7, where your property would be sold and they'd get your money now.

WHAT IF YOUR PROPERTY IS WORTH MORE THAN YOU THOUGHT?

In a Chapter 7 case, you might find that some of your property is sold when you didn't expect it to be. Of course, you had figured out what your property was worth even before you decided to file bankruptcy, let alone when you filed. But suppose you were wrong.

For example, say you said your house was worth a certain amount, based on conversations with the neighbors about recent home sales. But when you get to the creditors' meeting, the trustee says, "I'm familiar with that neighborhood, and I think your house is worth a lot more than what you put down." The trustee might decide to send an appraiser over to take a look. If the appraised value comes back showing you have more equity in your house than you're allowed to keep under the laws in your state, you could lose your house.

That's why it's so important to get a realistic assessment of your property before you file. If you had arranged for a realtor to give you a market analysis, you would have been prepared when the trustee questioned the value you had put down in your paperwork. The trustee is less likely to want a separate appraisal if he or she can see that there is a reasonable basis for your figure, rather than anecdotal evidence from the neighbors. Also, the trustee will be reassured that you have documentation that a professional had checked out the place.

Besides not wanting any surprises, it's important to put down realistic values because you don't want to raise any doubts about your credibility. If you drastically lowball the value of your house, the trustee will wonder what else you might be hiding. He or she may then want to go over your paperwork more carefully and question you on everything.

Remember, you don't want to be special in the eyes of the bankruptcy trustee. You want your case to cross that desk just once and be on its way.

ATTRACTING UNWANTED ATTENTION FROM THE AUTHORITIES

BESIDES THE trustee appointed to oversee your case, you may also have to worry about the Office of the United States Trustee. People who work there are on the look-out for fraud. They read all the petitions, looking for anything that may be out of the ordinary. Occasionally, an employee of the trustee's office will show up at the creditors' meeting and question the debtor about the information in their schedules.

One area that attracts the attention of the United States Trustee is the amount and nature of the debt. A petition showing $150,000 worth of medical bills won't raise an eyebrow. But that amount in credit card debt will raise a flag, especially if the part of the petition showing property reveals that the debtor doesn't own anything of value. You'd better be prepared to explain where the money went.

There are explanations, of course. First, it's amazing how fast credit card balances can grow when no payments are being made. The companies keep tacking on the late fees and over-limit fees as well as interest. If the debts are old, the balances will be several times higher than the sum of the original charges.

The money may have been spent on cash advances in order to pay the rent while the debtor was out of work. Doctors and health clinics accept credit cards. The money may have gone to meet medical expenses but they show up as credit card debt. You might be asked to produce credit statements for the several months before you filed to show how the credit card balances got so high.

In recent years, I've heard more people sheepishly admit that much of the debt was incurred while gambling. Casinos accept credit cards these days. In fact, machines are thoughtfully placed on the gambling floor to make it easier to get cash. You don't even have to have one of those credit cards that allow cash withdrawals with the use of a personal identification number. On these machines, no PIN is required. Just pop in your credit card and the machine spits out cash.

I think that's unconscionable. Yes, people are responsible for their own actions. But gambling can be an addiction, just like drugs or alcohol. It shouldn't be made this easy for people who have a problem. It's amazing how much debt one can run up in just one wild and losing weekend in Atlantic City or Las Vegas.

If the debt is largely attributed to gambling losses, and those losses occurred within twelve months before the filing of the petition, the debtor should have listed that in the Statement of Financial Affairs. It would have been written in response to the question about losses due to fire, theft, or gambling. The losses should be put down, even if the gambling was illegal. Fortunately, the paperwork doesn't ask for the name and address of your bookie. It just wants a description of the property, its value, the date of loss, and the circumstances under which the property was lost.

You can't hide it, even if it reflects badly on you. You signed those papers under penalty of perjury. You're stuck with telling the truth.

THE WORST-CASE SCENARIO—WHAT COULD HAPPEN IF YOU LIE

AND THAT leads me to the worst thing that can happen in a bankruptcy case. You can go to prison. This almost never happens, but it is a possibility. It is bankruptcy fraud for a debtor to hide assets or debts, or otherwise lie in the paperwork or during a hearing. The jurisdiction in which I practice actually has a sign, prominently displayed in the front of the hearing room, which advises that the FBI investigates bankruptcy fraud.

Consider the case of a California doctor, Robert A. Grant, who filed for bankruptcy protection in 1995. He neglected to mention some of his assets, including eighty acres of land and $4.5 million in liquid assets that he had stashed in the names of various corporations and trusts, held in other people's names but really managed by him.

After the bankruptcy was over, the property was transferred back to him. Dr. Grant pleaded guilty to bankruptcy fraud, as well as conspiracy and money laundering. He was sentenced to serve thirty-three months in prison.

I'm not telling you this to frighten you. Prison time for bankruptcy is a rare occurrence. Prosecutors have to prove that the information was deliberately hidden rather than the result of an innocent oversight. Usually, a fair amount of money is at stake. But no matter what your situation, you need to be completely honest with the court. Lying could result in the revocation of your discharge—and worse.

PART FIVE

LIFE AFTER BANKRUPTCY

CHAPTER EIGHTEEN

CLEANING UP YOUR CREDIT REPORT

Actor Gary Coleman, known as a child for his work in the TV sitcom Diff'rent Strokes, *was thirty-one when he filed a Chapter 7 bankruptcy, listing $72,000 in debts. He had $100 in the bank when he filed, as well as three firearms and a model train collection.*

In 2003, Coleman was among dozens of people to run for governor of California. He lost to a taller actor.

Bankruptcy does not mean the end of your credit life. You might feel you never want credit again. But that may be shortsighted. There may come a time in your life when you want or need credit, so it's a good idea to think about it sooner rather than later.

The following are a few suggestions that might help. Now, the credit business is always changing, so I can't guarantee that anything I'm telling you will work months or years from now. But as of right now, here are a few ideas that my clients have found helpful:

1. ***Find out what potential creditors will find out about you.*** When you go to buy a car or apply for a store charge card, what will those creditors be told about your credit history? Get a copy of your credit report. There are three major

credit-reporting agencies that are used by most creditors. Amazingly enough, they won't all have the same information. To be very thorough about this, I suggest you get a copy of your report from each of them. In fact, I believe all consumers—whether they've been through a bankruptcy or not—should pull at least one copy of their credit reports every year. There are often small mistakes that should be corrected immediately.

There's now a law in effect designed to provide consumers with a free credit report once a year. The Fair Credit Reporting Act requires all three credit-reporting agencies to provide free copies upon request.

To order a report, call 877-322-8228 or go to www.annualcreditreport.com. You may order a report from one, two, or three agencies. You're allowed a free copy from each of them every twelve months.

You may qualify for a free report even more often under certain circumstances. For example, if you have been denied credit or a job in the past sixty days based on information in a report, that credit-reporting agency must provide you with a free copy. You are also entitled, by law, to a free report if you certify that you are unemployed and looking for work, you're on welfare, or if your report is inaccurate because of fraud. In those cases, contact the agency directly rather than the central number or Web site. Their sites are www.transunion.com; www.equifax .com; and www.experian.com.

2. ***Find out your credit score.*** A credit score reduces your credit history to a number that creditors can use to make a quick decision on whether to lend to you. The most commonly used scoring system is called FICO, because it was developed by Fair Isaac and Company.

It's a number between 300 and 900, with 300 the worst and 900 the best. Exactly how the number is calculated is a secret. Generally, the system considers several factors in determining your credit-worthiness:

* Your payment history, whether you pay your bills on time. Your score will be lowered by late payments, referrals to collection agencies, and yes, whether you filed for bankruptcy protection.
* How much debt you have at any given time. It's not only the amount, but also how it compares to your limits. You will lose points if you are near or at your credit limits. The more cards you've maxed out, the worse your score will be.
* The length of your credit history. Obviously, having a longtime account that

you've always paid on time will improve your score. Creditors consider the way you've handled credit in the past as a good indication of how you'll behave in the future.

- The number and kinds of accounts you have. Too many cards could lower your score. Your score may be affected if you have loans from finance companies that charge a high interest rate. That's a red flag that you may have had trouble getting credit in the past.
- Part of the score is based on the number of "inquiries" on your report—the number of companies checking into your credit. This can indicate that you're applying for credit from several sources, another red flag that you may be in financial trouble.

Of course, companies will check out your credit without you knowing about it. Those "you've been approved" offers are not random. Companies monitor your credit report to determine if they want to send you a solicitation.

Inquiries for that purpose are not supposed to count against you, since you didn't initiate them. But it might not be a bad idea to try to reduce that anyway. At this point in your life, you don't need any more junk mail promising easy credit. The credit bureaus have set up a toll free number (888-567-8688) for people to call to request that they no longer be sent such prescreened solicitations.

3. *Check your report and score carefully.* Once you have received your credit reports, including your credit score, your real work begins. The first thing to do once you get your credit report is to read it carefully. It's tempting to jump right to the creditors but take your time and read through the thing line by line. Check your name, Social Security number—everything.

Next, check each account to see if it is accurate. It should show the debts as being discharged in bankruptcy. Quite often, there will be a debt or two still there, listed as something you owe. Be on the lookout for any debts that are listed twice. The report should show just the original account, not every single collection agency that once handled that account. It's common for the same debt to surface in various forms, making it look like you owed more than you did. I repeat— there are always mistakes on these reports. That's because the credit reporting agencies simply report the information they have and the creditors have no real incentive to let them know the debts have been discharged in bankruptcy. So, you'll have to do it yourself.

4. *Dispute any inaccuracies.* All the credit-reporting agencies include instructions on how to dispute a debt. Fill it out completely and send it in. Or write your own. I've provided some examples in Appendix VI, on page 195.

Be sure to include your bankruptcy papers (a copy of the hearing notice, the discharge order, and the page where the disputed account is listed). By law, the credit-reporting agencies must investigate and correct misinformation. You should also write to the creditor itself, requesting that the information be corrected. Provide all the same information, including copies of the discharge, etc. Bury them in paperwork!

This might take more than one attempt. Are you familiar with that arcade game called "Whack-A-Mole"? The object is to hit a mole with a hammer when it pops up through a hole. As soon as you whack one mole, another one pops up somewhere else. Fixing mistakes on your credit report is a lot like that. Just when you get one bad thing removed, another one pops up. You must be ever vigilant.

If a creditor is reluctant to correct information, you might try a stronger letter. I have one in which I point out that it is a violation of a court order to try to collect a debt after the bankruptcy is filed. A creditor who refuses to remove erroneous information could be seen as trying to collect that debt. It can be helpful to remind a creditor of the consequences of defying the court.

If a creditor continues to list a debt as owed when the debt has been discharged in bankruptcy, you could even sue under the Fair Credit Reporting Act. I know some bankruptcy lawyers who are starting to branch out into filing these lawsuits in order to force creditors to be fair. This can also result in a cash settlement for their clients. These days, having inaccurate information on your credit report could be disastrous. Courts will award damages, and may order the creditor to pay for the cost of the litigation.

Credit reporting agencies also allow you to include a short statement to be included in your file. This would allow you to put your own spin on the circumstances that led to filing bankruptcy. Keep it brief. Potential creditors don't want to hear your life story. Don't be whiny. Simply state the facts. Get someone whose opinion you trust to look it over before you send it in. Everyone needs an editor.

All this work might tempt you to hire one of those services that advertise that they can fix up your credit report for a fee. Be careful. Some of them even claim they can get rid of a bankruptcy. There is no legal way to do this. A bankruptcy will remain on your credit report for ten years. I repeat—there's no legal way to get rid of it before then.

There may be some legitimate credit-repair companies out there, but even they can't do anything that you can't do for yourself. It might take some time, but you'd have to spend some time to make sure the people you're hiring are legit, so you may as well do it yourself.

There are better ways to spend your money to rebuild your credit.

CHAPTER NINETEEN

ESTABLISHING NEW CREDIT

The singer with the baggy pants, MC Hammer, was one of the first rap artists to catch the attention of mainstream fans, with his hit single "U Can't Touch This." He made millions with his records and tours. But he spent even more than he earned. The cable music station VH1 reported that Hammer had an entourage large enough to successfully invade Switzerland.

Hammer declared bankruptcy protection in 1996, losing his mansion in the process. The experience changed him. He became religious and released an album of gospel music. After the September 11th attacks, he came out with an album showcasing new artists, donating part of the profits to 9-11 charities. More recently Hammer landed some work in television including a commercial spoofing his financial troubles.

ONCE your credit reports are accurate, you can move on to the next step. Bankruptcy is not the end of the world for you financially. You can recover from this. Despite those ads from credit-counseling services that claim that bankruptcy is a "ten-year mistake," you can certainly get credit again far sooner.

My very unofficial, unscientific findings are that one can even buy a house two or three years after filing bankruptcy. The reason that I know is that I have former clients call me up and ask for another copy of their bankruptcy papers. They're buying a house, the mortgage company needs to see the bankruptcy paperwork, and they've lost it.

Hang on to your paperwork, both the entire petition and the final order that comes after your case is over. You will need it for something some day. Part of starting over after going through this process is to take this seriously. It's possible you got into financial difficulties partly because you weren't careful about your finances. Resolve to be more organized and keep a close watch on everything that affects your money.

Another way I know that it's possible to get credit after a bankruptcy is my repeat customers. Under current law, you can file a Chapter 7 bankruptcy just eight years after your last one. Obviously, that's not something I recommend but it does show how much trouble one can get into in that time.

Often a client who comes back to me for a second time is someone who experienced a major disaster. I had a client who was forced to file again after being in a car accident that was his fault. His insurance had lapsed and so the other person's insurance company was suing him for a zillion dollars. He simply couldn't pay it back. He had no way to fight a judgment and would most likely have ended up losing 25 percent of his take-home pay forever.

Another common reason for a repeat filing is huge medical bills. Just one uninsured weekend in a hospital would probably drive a lot of people into bankruptcy. Even people who are careful with their money and always save would have trouble absorbing that kind of hit.

Even those clients who had to file again for such reasons also had some credit card debt. Somehow, everyone manages to get a credit card.

So, how do they do it? First off, after filing bankruptcy, you are going to get some unsolicited credit card offers. Be very careful. Many of them are scams, which I'll discuss in the next chapter.

You are actually a good risk after going through bankruptcy. You don't have any debt and you can't file bankruptcy again for eight years.

One way to get credit again is to apply for a secured credit card. It will look just like a regular VISA or MasterCard, but it's really paid up front. You send some money to the credit card company, say $500, and then you can charge up to that amount. These are no-risk deals for the banks, since if you don't pay as agreed, they can simply take it from your deposit. Eventually, your credit limit may be raised above the amount that you deposited. Some will even convert to an unsecured card some day.

I can't tell you exactly where to go to find a bank that offers a secured credit card.

The credit card industry changes constantly and anything I type today is liable to be outdated by the time you read it. With the Internet, there's lots of information out there and you should be able to find it.

Just make sure that the company will report the account as a regular account, not a secured credit card account. There's no point in dealing with a company that won't give you what you want—a good credit reference. An account *described* as secured won't do that.

Similarly, banks and credit unions offer check-cashing cards that look like a regular credit card. You can use them in places that accept credit cards but the amount comes directly out of your account. They might help you in situations where you need a credit card. But they won't help rebuild your credit.

Secured credit cards work somewhat the same way, in that you're not getting into more debt. But, if you chose wisely, a secured card can improve your credit. As with any agreement, make sure you read it carefully and know exactly what you're getting into. If there's an application fee, find out if it will be refunded if your application is denied. There may also be a yearly maintenance fee. Find out the interest rate on outstanding balances and how it's calculated. You don't want to get into a situation in which your deposit would be eaten up by fees or interest.

Another possible source of credit would be a local merchant. Some small stores offer credit, especially if you put down a large down payment. Make sure the store will report your on-time payments to the credit bureaus, and don't buy something just to get a credit reference. Part of your new life of financial responsibility is only buying things you need, and only after careful consideration. Maybe some day, you'll be wealthy enough to be able to buy something frivolous on a whim. That day is not today. Even if you have the cash, you're better off saving it so that you can offer a large down payment when you do need to buy something on credit.

For example, you'll need to get another car someday. In an ideal world, you could simply write a check on your savings account. But most of us can't do that. Many car dealerships will offer car loans soon after a bankruptcy, but you'll pay a higher interest rate. If you can bring a big down payment to the table, you'll be in a much better position to negotiate a better interest rate. It's a matter of shopping around. Some places are more reasonable than others.

One place to check for a car loan is your own bank or credit union, assuming they were not affected by your bankruptcy. If you have a good history with them, not bouncing checks, etc., they may offer more favorable terms than your local car dealer. In fact, it's probably a good idea to go shopping for the financing before hitting the showrooms. It would be helpful to know what you can reasonably afford before you start imagining yourself behind a particular wheel.

Do your research on cars, as well. Even if I had the expertise—which I don't—I don't have room here to go into everything that you should consider when shopping for a car. This is a huge purchase and should be completed only after a lot of consideration. Read up on smart ways to do this. I will give you one piece of advice—never buy a car when you have a rambunctious toddler in tow. Trust me on this.

Another area where credit is important is in leasing a home or an apartment. Again, you'll have to shop around. There are some places that won't want to deal with people who've filed bankruptcy. Other places aren't so picky. Be up front about it. They're going to find out anyway. You ought to be prepared to explain how it happened.

I have written letters for former clients who run into trouble with resident managers. I write that it was my professional opinion that the client had no choice but to file bankruptcy. I personalize it somewhat, to include pertinent information such as a divorce or job loss. I end by saying I expect the client will successfully reestablish her credit in the future.

There is no legal component to this letter, of course. But it's on my lawyer letterhead and seems to help. Resident managers can be bureaucrats like everyone else. Some like to have a piece of paper in the file from a lawyer to justify their decision.

One way to start building your credit again is to talk someone into being a cosigner for you. Of course, it should be someone who has good credit. As a practical matter, it should also be someone who hasn't read this book! I always advise people to be very wary of cosigning for anyone, especially someone with financial troubles.

I've had numerous clients over the years who found themselves in my office telling their tale of woe because they had cosigned for someone. Many of them were older women who had been induced to cosign credit cards for their grown children. The "kids" don't pay but also don't warn Mom that trouble is coming. By the time she realizes there's a problem, the balances are sky-high, bloated by late fees, over-limit charges, and jacked-up interest rates. Sometimes, she finds out the account is in default only when she's been served with court papers that she's being sued.

I can't understand how people could do that to their mothers. But they do. So everyone should be cautious about being a cosigner for anyone, even one's own flesh and blood. Signing any loan application makes you equally responsible. It doesn't matter whose name is listed first, whether you're the "applicant" or the "coapplicant." Credit card companies don't care. They'll go after either or both of you to get their money.

Having said all that, if you can talk someone else into doing this, you could get credit faster. Make sure you make all the payments on time. This isn't just to protect your mom but to accomplish your goal of obtaining a good credit report. There's certainly no point in getting a credit reference and then messing it up.

Don't apply for too much credit at once. Inquiries also show up on your report. Potential creditors get spooked if they see that you're trying to get credit all over town. If you apply somewhere and you get turned down, wait a bit until you apply to some other company. In the meantime, ask the company that rejected you to reconsider. Many companies have a "reapplication" department, which will take another look. Make sure you include a short statement explaining why you had to file bankruptcy and your prospects for a more financially stable future.

Once you do obtain a credit card, keep it active. Charge something small every month but then pay the bill as soon as it comes in.

Even once your credit report has improved, don't take on more credit cards than you need just because you can. No one needs more than one or two major credit cards, in addition to a gas or department store card. Getting more cards than that is just asking for trouble.

Remember that credit is certainly a fact of life in our society and can be a helpful tool for you to control your finances. Just don't ever let it control you.

CHAPTER TWENTY

LOOK OUT FOR THE SCAMS

Showman P. T. Barnum is quoted as saying "There's a sucker born every minute." He claimed he was swindled when he invested in a clock company. He listed half a million dollars of debts when he filed bankruptcy, a huge amount in 1856.

In 1871, he started a circus he called "The Greatest Show on Earth." Ten years later, he and his biggest competitor, James A. Bailey, joined forces to form the Barnum and Bailey Circus.

ONE way to spot the scams is to count the exclamation points. Stay away from the offers that shout "YOU ARE APPROVED!" "YOU CAN'T BE TURNED DOWN!" or "BAD CREDIT? NO CREDIT? NO PROBLEM!!!"

If you respond to one of those ads, you're likely to get a number of results, none of them what you're looking for.

You might be asked to pay an application fee that could run into the hundreds of dollars. Sometimes the company will suggest that you authorize it to deduct the amount directly from your checking account, on any date in the future that you specify. But instead of waiting for the specified date, the company cashes it right away. That's the last thing it does for you, or rather, to you.

Other companies will give you something in return but it won't be useful. Some simply mail you a list of companies that offer credit cards.

You might receive a credit card with a mail order catalogue. You can only use it to buy merchandise from the catalogue. Some say you *will* get a regular credit card, but only after you buy $500 worth of merchandise. You already know you've been scammed at this point. You're sure not going to buy a bunch of overpriced stuff you don't want on the chance the company will follow through.

But, you say, this company offers a money-back guarantee. Good luck getting your money back. Professional scam artists will do or say anything to separate you from your money. Sure, they can give you a guarantee that they have no intention of honoring. And don't be fooled if they pass you over to a "supervisor" to confirm the terms of your guarantee, even if they say they're tape recording your conversation to ensure that they're on the up-and-up. Remember, they can say anything they want. An unscrupulous company can run the scam for awhile, rake in the money, and then close up shop with no forwarding address.

Even if you can track them down, they're not likely to simply give back your money. Of course you could sue them if you could figure out where they are. But the many hoops you'd have to go through to find out makes that option unattractive. At some point, you'll decide the effort you're expending isn't worth it. That's what they're counting on. So be very careful before you respond to one of those ads.

Sometimes, it's the call itself the scammers are after. You are instructed to dial a 900 number to process your application. Unlike 800 or 888 numbers, you pay for the call. Who knows where you're calling? It might take a while for the "creditor" to get all the information it wants and you could end up with a hefty phone bill. And surprise, surprise—you never get a credit card out of the deal.

Here are a few signs an offer is a scam:

- The ad assures you that there will be no credit check. Any legitimate company is going to want to see your credit report, even those that lend money to people with less than perfect credit.
- You have to call a 900 number to apply.
- The ad absolutely guarantees that you will be approved. No legitimate company will do that. This is a double warning sign if the ad specifies that you are absolutely approved for a large credit limit such as $2,500.

* The card is offered by a company that claims to be in the business of credit repair, especially if the name implies that it's a not-for-profit operation. The real credit repair agencies are more interested in getting people out of debt, not into debt.
* Any offer that prompts you to say, "Wow! That sounds too good to be true." You know the old saying about that. This is another one of those situations in which you should listen to your gut.

Even legitimate credit companies sometimes offer useless services.

For example, some companies offer "credit insurance," to protect your card in case it gets stolen. The offer assures that you would not be responsible for any bogus charges if you notify the company right away. Sometimes, the company will offer this service free for three months but then charge you a monthly fee, which it will helpfully take by hitting your credit card automatically.

The problem is that under federal law, you are protected in the event someone steals your card for any purchase over $50, if you notify the company right away. Many companies will forgive that $50 anyway.

Another worthless service is credit disability insurance. Again, the idea sounds good. If you are disabled, your minimum payments are covered until you can get back on your feet.

Maybe there are some companies out there who honor such plans. I've never heard of one. I've heard from many, many clients that when they had a disability, their claim was denied.

Don't be discouraged by all these stories of bad guys out to get you. There are some decent companies out there. It's up to you to figure out which ones they are.

Once you do get some credit, use it wisely. Resolve to never again get in the position of waking with cold sweats or letting the answering machine pick up because you have no way to pay your bills.

Your best friend right now is your good common sense. You know now how easy it can be to get in over your head. You know that nothing you buy on a whim will bring you more pleasure than a savings account and little or no debt.

I'm reminded of that great Jimmy Buffett song, "Permanent Reminder of a Temporary Feeling." He was talking about things like tattoos, but he could just as well have been talking about having huge credit card balances with nothing to show for them. You know from your own experience how easily that can happen and how stupid you feel later on.

Your other best friend is time. We have short attention spans here in the United States. We reinvent ourselves all the time. You can tell from some of the little anecdotes about famous people that I've included that there is life after bankruptcy. Okay, some of them aren't exactly role models. But their experiences show you can go on after bankruptcy and be successful.

Make the most of your fresh start.

APPENDIX I

WORKSHEET 1
ASSESSING YOUR DEBTS

DEBTS

NAME OF CREDITOR	BALANCE	INTEREST RATE	MINIMUM PAYMENT	PERCENTAGE OF MINIMUM PAYMENT THAT GOES TO PRINCIPAL
_____	_____	_____	_____	_____
_____	_____	_____	_____	_____
_____	_____	_____	_____	_____
_____	_____	_____	_____	_____
_____	_____	_____	_____	_____
_____	_____	_____	_____	_____
_____	_____	_____	_____	_____
_____	_____	_____	_____	_____
_____	_____	_____	_____	_____
_____	_____	_____	_____	_____
_____	_____	_____	_____	_____
_____	_____	_____	_____	_____

Balance Total: _____   *Minimum Total:* _____   *Portion Total:* _____

Divide the balance total by the minimum total to figure out how many months it would take to pay your debts at your current rate. This is a rough figure: Remember that interest continues to accrue.

WORKSHEET 2
MONTHLY INCOME

If you are paid every other week:

Multiply _____ by 26, then divide by 12   =   _____
   (take-home pay)

If you are paid twice a month:

Multiply _____ by 2   =   _____
   (take-home pay)

If you are paid once a month, enter the amount here: _____
                  (take-home pay)

If your pay varies from month to month:

Add several take-home paychecks, and then divide by the number of paychecks to get an average figure. For example, if you have six pay stubs, divide the total by six. Then proceed as above.

WORKSHEET 3
MONTHLY EXPENSES

Rent or mortgage   _____

Utilities:

        Electricity and heating fuel   _____

        Telephone (include long distance and cell)   _____

        Cable and Internet   _____

Food   _____

Clothing   _____

Laundry and dry cleaning   _____

Medical and dental   _____

Transportation:

        Car payment   _____

        Gas and repairs   _____

        Public transportation   _____

Insurance:

        Car   _____

        Health (not deducted from pay)   _____

        Life   _____

        Homeowner's or rental   _____

Taxes (not deducted from pay)   _____

Child and spousal support   _____

Miscellaneous:

        Charity   _____

        Recreation   _____

Home maintenance   _____
Children's expenses   _____

Other regular monthly expenses   _____

                                                    _____

Total monthly expenses: _____
Total monthly income: _____

WORKSHEET 4
CALCULATING YOUR ASSETS

ASSET	VALUE (AFTER DEDUCTING ANY LIENS)	COULD YOU SELL?
House	_____	_____
Car	_____	_____
Car #2	_____	_____
Furniture	_____	_____
Computer equipment	_____	_____
Stereo equipment	_____	_____
Memorabilia	_____	_____
Stocks and bonds	_____	_____
Insurance policy	_____	_____

Appendix II

State-by-State Homestead Exemptions

State	Home Exemption	"Wildcard" Exemption
Alabama	$5,000	$3,000
Alaska	$64,800	none
Arizona	$100,000	none
Arkansas	$2,500	$500
California	$50,000	$800
Colorado	$45,000	none
Connecticut	$75,000	$1,000
Delaware	none	$5,000
District of Columbia	100%	none
Florida	100%	$1,000
Georgia	$10,000	$5,000
Hawaii	$30,000	none
Idaho	$50,000	$800
Illinois	$7,500	$2,000
Indiana	$7,500	$4,000
Iowa	100%	none
Kansas	100%	none
Kentucky	$5,000	$1,000
Louisiana	$55,000	none
Maine	$35,000	$400
Maryland	$2,500	$3,000
Massachusetts	$300,000	none
Michigan	$3,500	none
Minnesota	$200,000	none
Mississippi	$75,000	$250

STATE	HOME EXEMPTION	"WILDCARD" EXEMPTION
Missouri	$15,000	$850
Montana	$100,000	none
Nebraska	$12,500	$2,500
Nevada	$125,000	none
New Hampshire	$100,000	$1,000
New Jersey	none	$1,000
New Mexico	$30,000	$500
New York	$10,000	none
North Carolina	$10,000	$3,500
North Dakota	$80,000	$5,000
Ohio	$5,000	$400
Oklahoma	100%	none
Oregon	$25,000	$400
Pennsylvania	none	$300
Rhode Island	$150,000	none
South Carolina	$5,000	none
South Dakota	$30,000	$6,000
Tennessee	$5,000	$4,000
Texas	100%	none
Utah	$20,000	none
Vermont	$75,000	$400
Virginia	none	$5,000
Washington	$40,000	$1,000
West Virginia	$25,000	$1,000
Wisconsin	$40,000	none
Wyoming	$10,000	none

Some states allow people in bankruptcy to use the federal exemptions instead. The federal homestead exemption is $18,450 and the wildcard is $925. Please note that the above figures were accurate when I wrote them. You'll need to look them up for yourself to see if there have been any changes since then.

APPENDIX III

MEDIAN INCOME FOR FAMILY OF FOUR—BY STATE

(Please note: These figures were the most recent provided by the U.S. Census Bureau as of publication of this book. You'll need to find more current information for your state and family size before making any decisions. Go to www.census.gov.)

Alabama	$55,448
Alaska	$72,110
Arizona	$58,206
Arkansas	$48,353
California	$67,814
Colorado	$71,559
Connecticut	$86,001
Delaware	$72,780
District of Colombia	$56,067
Florida	$58,605
Georgia	$62,294
Hawaii	$71,732
Idaho	$53,376
Illinois	$72,368
Indiana	$65,009
Iowa	$64,341
Kansas	$64,215
Kentucky	$53,198
Louisiana	$50,529
Maine	$59,596
Maryland	$82,363
Massachusetts	$82,561
Michigan	$68,602

Minnesota	$76,733
Mississippi	$46,570
Missouri	$64,128
Montana	$49,124
Nebraska	$63,625
Nevada	$63,005
New Hampshire	$79,339
New Jersey	$87,412
New Mexico	$45,867
New York	$69,354
North Carolina	$56,712
North Dakota	$57,092
Ohio	$66,066
Oklahoma	$50,216
Oregon	$61,570
Pennsylvania	$68,578
Rhode Island	$71,098
South Carolina	$56,433
South Dakota	$59,272
Tennessee	$55,401
Texas	$54,554
Utah	$62,032
Vermont	$65,876
Virginia	$71,697
Washington	$69,130
West Virginia	$46,169
Wisconsin	$69,010
Wyoming	$56,065

APPENDIX IV

BANKRUPTCY WORKSHEET

Today's Date: _____

PERSONAL INFORMATION

Name: _____
          (FIRST)   (MIDDLE)   (LAST)

SSN: _____

Spouse's Name: _____
                  (FIRST)   (MIDDLE)   (LAST)

Spouse's SSN: _____

Address: _____

County: _____

How long have you lived at your current address? _____

List any other names that you have used in the last five years:

    (H) _____

    (W) _____

List other addresses for the past two years:

_____
(COMPLETE ADDRESS PLEASE)

_____

Marital Status: Married _____ Divorced _____ Separated _____ Single _____

Have you filed bankruptcy before? _____ If so, list location where filed, case number,

date filed, and discharge date: _____

PROPERTY INFORMATION

List all real estate in which you have an interest:

    Type of property: _____

    Address: _____

    Market value: _____

    Type of property: _____

    Address: _____

    Market value: _____

How much cash do you normally have on hand? _____

List all checking accounts, savings accounts, certificates of deposit, credit union accounts, etc., that you have, along with the name(s) on the account:

_____

(BANKING INSTITUTION NAME)

_____

(TYPE OF ACCOUNT)   (AMOUNT)

_____

(BANKING INSTITUTION NAME)

_____

(TYPE OF ACCOUNT)   (AMOUNT)

Security deposits with public utilities, telephone companies, landlords, and others:

_____

(NAME)   (AMOUNT)

List estimated yard sale value of any of the following property you own:

TV	_____	VCR	_____
Other electronics	_____	Stereo	_____
Home computer	_____	Sofa	_____
Tables	_____	Chairs	_____
Lamps	_____	Beds and bedding	_____
Dressers	_____	Dishes	_____
Silverware	_____	Appliances	_____

Tools	_____	Carpets	_____
Books	_____	Pictures	_____
Antiques and collectibles	_____	Wearing apparel	_____
Wedding/engagement rings	_____	Other jewelry	_____
Sports equipment	_____	Hobby equipment	_____
Animals	_____		

List any 401(k), IRA, ERISA, Keogh, or other pension or profit sharing plans:

_____

(INSTITUTION NAME)   (AMOUNT IN ACCOUNT)

_____

(INSTITUTION NAME)   (AMOUNT IN ACCOUNT)

Do you own any stocks, bonds, annuities, etc.? If so, list the company and how many shares:

_____

_____

_____

Are you expecting any tax refunds? If so, who from and how much:

_____

Do you own any insurance policies with a cash value? (a "whole life" policy you can borrow against, not the "term life" you get through work):

_____

Motor vehicles:

Make, year, and value _____ Mileage _____

Make, year, and value _____ Mileage _____

Make, year, and value _____ Mileage _____

Please list any other items of value you own, not previously listed:

_____

_____

_____

Does anyone owe you money? If so, who and how much:

_____

_____

CREDITOR INFORMATION

Do you owe any taxes? List name, address, year, and amount:

Federal: _____

_____

State: _____

_____

Other taxes: _____

_____

Do you owe any child or spousal support? List name, address, and amount:

_____

_____

SECURED CREDITORS

Name: _____

Address: _____

Description of property: _____

Account number: _____   When did you get this loan? _____

Market value: _____   Amount owed: _____

Do you want to keep (reaffirm) the property? _____ yes _____ no

Monthly payment: _____

Name: _____

Address: _____

Description of property: _____

Account number: _____   When did you get this loan? _____

Market value: _____   Amount owed: _____

Do you want to keep (reaffirm) the property? _____ yes _____ no

Monthly payment: _____

Name: _____

Address: _____

Description of property: _____

Account number: _____   When did you get this loan? _____

Market value: _____   Amount owed: _____

Do you want to keep (reaffirm) the property? _____ yes _____ no

Monthly payment: _____

UNSECURED CREDITORS

Name: _____

Address: _____

Account number: _____   First used: _____

Last used: _____

Type of debt: _____   Amount owed: _____

Name: _____

Address: _____

Account number: _____   First used: _____

Last used: _____

Type of debt: _____   Amount owed: _____

Name: _____

Address: _____

Account number: _____   First used: _____

Last used: _____

Type of debt: _____   Amount owed: _____

Name: _____

Address: _____

Account number: _____   First used: _____

Last used: _____

Type of debt: _____   Amount owed: _____

Name: _____

Address: _____

Account number: _____   First used: _____

Last used: _____

Type of debt: _____   Amount owed: _____

Name: _____

Address: _____

Account number: _____   First used: _____

Last used: _____

Type of debt: _____   Amount owed: _____

Name: _____

Address: _____

Account number: _____   First used: _____

Last used: _____

Type of debt: _____   Amount owed: _____

Name: _____

Address: _____

Account number: _____   First used: _____

Last used: _____

Type of debt: _____   Amount owed: _____

Name: _____

Address: _____

Account number: _____   First used: _____

Last used: _____

Type of debt: _____   Amount owed: _____

Name: _____

Address: _____

Account number: _____   First used: _____

Last used: _____

Type of debt: _____   Amount owed: _____

Name: _____

Address: _____

Account number: _____   First used: _____

Last used: _____

Type of debt: _____   Amount owed: _____

Name: _____

Address: _____

Account number: _____   First used: _____

Last used: _____

Type of debt: _____   Amount owed: _____

MISCELLANEOUS FINANCIAL QUESTIONS

Are you obligated under a lease for a home, car, etc.? List what you lease, and the name and address of the person or company you lease from. (They won't be notified.)

_____

_____

_____

Is there anyone else, other than your spouse, liable for any of the debts? If so, list their name and address, and the name of the creditor:

_____

_____

_____

Estimated gross income so far this year: (Husband) _____ (Wife) _____

Estimated gross income last year: (Husband) _____ (Wife) _____

Estimated gross income two years ago: (Husband) _____   (Wife) _____

Did you receive income from any other source in the last two years (such as Social Security, support, or pension)? If so, list source, year, and amount:

_____

_____

List all suits and garnishments within one year:

_____
(CASE NO.)   (COURT)

_____
(CASE NO.)   (COURT)

List all repossessions, foreclosures, and returns within one year. Provide name and address of creditor, date, description, and value of property:

_____

_____

List any gifts or charitable contributions over $200 made within the last year:

_____

Have you lost any property from fire, theft, or gambling within one year? If so, list description, circumstances, whether covered by insurance, and date of loss:

_____

Have you paid or agreed to pay any other attorney for bankruptcy within one year? If so, list name, address, date of payment, and amount:

_____

List any property you transferred in the past year and whom it was transferred to:

_____

List any safe deposit boxes. Include name and address of bank, names of who has access, and description of contents:

_____

List any accounts you closed in the past year and the final balance:

_____

Are you holding any property for another person? If so, list name, address, and description of property:

_____

Have you paid any single creditor more than $600 in the past 90 days?

_____

INCOME INFORMATION

(PLEASE PROVIDE A COPY OF YOUR MOST RECENT PAY STUB)

What is your current occupation?:

(Husband): _____
(TITLE/POSITION)

(Wife): _____
(TITLE/POSITION)

Name and address of current employer:

(Husband): _____

_____

Length of employment: _____
(Wife): _____

_____

Length of employment: _____
How often are you paid? (Husband): _____ (Wife): _____
List names and birth dates of dependents:

_____

_____

Did you have your own business in the last six years? If so, provide the details, such as name, description, tax ID number, and starting and ending dates:

_____

_____

MONTHLY EXPENSES

Rent or mortgage: ____   Real estate tax: ____

Insurance: ____   Condo/homeowner's assn. fee: ____

Maintenance: ____

Utilities:

Electricity and heating fuel: ____   Water: ____

Telephone: ____   Cable: ____

Other: ____

Food: ____   Clothing: ____

Laundry/dry cleaning: ____   Medical/dental expenses: ____

Recreation: ____   Charity: ____

Transportation:

Car payment: ____   Gas: ____

Repairs: ____   Public transportation: ____

Insurance:

Health: ____   Life: ____

Auto: ____   Renters': ____

Taxes: ____   Support paid to others: ____

Miscellaneous:

Business expenses: ____   Day care: ____

Gifts: ____   Children's expenses: ____

Hair cuts: ____   Stamps: ____

Anything else you can think of?: _____

APPENDIX V

SAMPLE BANKRUPTCY PETITION

FORM B1	United States Bankruptcy Court Eastern District of Virginia	Voluntary Petition

Name of Debtor (if individual, enter Last, First, Middle): **Doe, Robert John**	Name of Joint Debtor (Spouse) (Last, First, Middle): **Doe, Dora Jean**
All Other Names used by the Debtor in the last 6 years (include married, maiden, and trade names):	All Other Names used by the Joint Debtor in the last 6 years (include married, maiden, and trade names):
Last four digits of Soc. Sec. No. / Complete EIN or other Tax I.D. No. (if more than one, state all): **xxx-xx-7803**	Last four digits of Soc. Sec. No. / Complete EIN or other Tax I.D. No. (if more than one, state all): **xxx-xx-4321**
Street Address of Debtor (No. & Street, City, State & Zip Code): **426 Happy Lane** **Fairfax, VA 22034**	Street Address of Joint Debtor (No. & Street, City, State & Zip Code): **426 Happy Lane** **Fairfax, VA 22034**
County of Residence or of the Principal Place of Business: **Fairfax**	County of Residence or of the Principal Place of Business: **Fairfax**
Mailing Address of Debtor (if different from street address):	Mailing Address of Joint Debtor (if different from street address):

Location of Principal Assets of Business Debtor (if different from street address above):

Information Regarding the Debtor (Check the Applicable Boxes)

Venue (Check any applicable box)
- ■ Debtor has been domiciled or has had a residence, principal place of business, or principal assets in this District for 180 days immediately preceding the date of this petition or for a longer part of such 180 days than in any other District.
- ☐ There is a bankruptcy case concerning debtor's affiliate, general partner, or partnership pending in this District.

Type of Debtor (Check all boxes that apply) ■ Individual(s) ☐ Railroad ☐ Corporation ☐ Stockbroker ☐ Partnership ☐ Commodity Broker ☐ Other_____ ☐ Clearing Bank	**Chapter or Section of Bankruptcy Code Under Which the Petition is Filed** (Check one box) ■ Chapter 7 ☐ Chapter 11 ☐ Chapter 13 ☐ Chapter 9 ☐ Chapter 12 ☐ Sec. 304 - Case ancillary to foreign proceeding
Nature of Debts (Check one box) ■ Consumer/Non-Business ☐ Business	**Filing Fee** (Check one box) ■ Full Filing Fee attached ☐ Filing Fee to be paid in installments (Applicable to individuals only.) Must attach signed application for the court's consideration
Chapter 11 Small Business (Check all boxes that apply) ☐ Debtor is a small business as defined in 11 U.S.C. § 101 ☐ Debtor is and elects to be considered a small business under 11 U.S.C. § 1121(e) (Optional)	certifying that the debtor is unable to pay fee except in installments. Rule 1006(b). See Official Form No. 3. ***** Sarah Solicitor *****

Statistical/Administrative Information (Estimates only)   THIS SPACE IS FOR COURT USE ONLY
- ☐ Debtor estimates that funds will be available for distribution to unsecured creditors.
- ■ Debtor estimates that, after any exempt property is excluded and administrative expenses paid, there will be no funds available for distribution to unsecured creditors.

Estimated Number of Creditors	1-15	16-49	50-99	100-199	200-999	1000-over
	■	☐	☐	☐	☐	☐

Estimated Assets							
$0 to $50,000	$50,001 to $100,000	$100,001 to $500,000	$500,001 to $1 million	$1,000,001 to $10 million	$10,000,001 to $50 million	$50,000,001 to $100 million	More than $100 million
■	☐	☐	☐	☐	☐	☐	☐

Estimated Debts							
$0 to $50,000	$50,001 to $100,000	$100,001 to $500,000	$500,001 to $1 million	$1,000,001 to $10 million	$10,000,001 to $50 million	$50,000,001 to $100 million	More than $100 million
☐	■	☐	☐	☐	☐	☐	☐

Voluntary Petition
This page must be completed and filed in every case)

Name of Debtor(s):	FORM B1, Page 2
Doe, Robert John	
Doe, Dora Jean	

Prior Bankruptcy Case Filed Within Last 6 Years (If more than one, attach additional sheet)

Location Where Filed: **- None -**	Case Number:	Date Filed:

Pending Bankruptcy Case Filed by any Spouse, Partner, or Affiliate of this Debtor (If more than one, attach additional sheet)

Name of Debtor: **None -**	Case Number:	Date Filed:
District:	Relationship:	Judge:

Signatures

Signature(s) of Debtor(s) (Individual/Joint)

I declare under penalty of perjury that the information provided in this petition is true and correct.
[If petitioner is an individual whose debts are primarily consumer debts and has chosen to file under chapter 7] I am aware that I may proceed under chapter 7, 11, 12, or 13 of title 11, United States Code, understand the relief available under each such chapter, and choose to proceed under chapter 7.
I request relief in accordance with the chapter of title 11, United States Code, specified in this petition.

X _____
Signature of Debtor **Robert John Doe**

X _____
Signature of Joint Debtor **Dora Jean Doe**

_____
Telephone Number (If not represented by attorney)

_____
Date

Signature of Attorney

X _____
Signature of Attorney for Debtor(s)
Sarah Solicitor
Printed Name of Attorney for Debtor(s)

Sarah Solicitor
Firm Name
9600 Litigation Lane
Alexandria, VA 22304

_____
Address

_____
Telephone Number

_____
Date

Signature of Debtor (Corporation/Partnership)

I declare under penalty of perjury that the information provided in this petition is true and correct, and that I have been authorized to file this petition on behalf of the debtor.
The debtor requests relief in accordance with the chapter of title 11, United States Code, specified in this petition.

X _____
Signature of Authorized Individual

_____
Printed Name of Authorized Individual

_____
Title of Authorized Individual

_____
Date

Exhibit A

(To be completed if debtor is required to file periodic reports (e.g., forms 10K and 10Q) with the Securities and Exchange Commission pursuant to Section 13 or 15(d) of the Securities Exchange Act of 1934 and is requesting relief under chapter 11)

☐ Exhibit A is attached and made a part of this petition.

Exhibit B

(To be completed if debtor is an individual whose debts are primarily consumer debts)

I, the attorney for the petitioner named in the foregoing petition, declare that I have informed the petitioner that [he or she] may proceed under chapter 7, 11, 12, or 13 of title 11, United States Code, and have explained the relief available under each such chapter.

X _____
Signature of Attorney for Debtor(s)   Date
Sarah Solicitor

Exhibit C

Does the debtor own or have possession of any property that poses a threat of imminent and identifiable harm to public health or safety?

☐ Yes, and Exhibit C is attached and made a part of this petition.
■ No

Signature of Non-Attorney Petition Preparer

I certify that I am a bankruptcy petition preparer as defined in 11 U.S.C. § 110, that I prepared this document for compensation, and that I have provided the debtor with a copy of this document.

_____
Printed Name of Bankruptcy Petition Preparer

_____
Social Security Number (Required by 11 U.S.C.§ 110(c).)

_____
Address

Names and Social Security numbers of all other individuals who prepared or assisted in preparing this document:

If more than one person prepared this document, attach additional sheets conforming to the appropriate official form for each person.

X _____
Signature of Bankruptcy Petition Preparer

_____
Date

A bankruptcy petition preparer's failure to comply with the provisions of title 11 and the Federal Rules of Bankruptcy Procedure may result in fines or imprisonment or both. 11 U.S.C. § 110; 18 U.S.C. § 156.

United States Bankruptcy Court
Eastern District of Virginia

In re   **Robert John Doe,**   Case No. _____
        Dora Jean Doe

_____,   Chapter _____ 7 _____
                                Debtors

SUMMARY OF SCHEDULES

Indicate as to each schedule whether that schedule is attached and state the number of pages in each. Report the totals from Schedules A, B, D, E, F, I, and J in the boxes provided. Add the amounts from Schedules A and B to determine the total amount of the debtor's assets. Add the amounts from Schedules D, E, and F to determine the total amount of the debtor's liabilities.

NAME OF SCHEDULE	ATTACHED (YES/NO)	NO. OF SHEETS	AMOUNTS SCHEDULED		
			ASSETS	LIABILITIES	OTHER
A - Real Property	Yes	1	0.00		
B - Personal Property	Yes	4	20,032.00		
C - Property Claimed as Exempt	Yes	2			
D - Creditors Holding Secured Claims	Yes	1		14,089.00	
E - Creditors Holding Unsecured Priority Claims	Yes	2		578.00	
F - Creditors Holding Unsecured Nonpriority Claims	Yes	3		60,238.00	
G - Executory Contracts and Unexpired Leases	Yes	1			
H - Codebtors	Yes	1			
I - Current Income of Individual Debtor(s)	Yes	1			2,856.
J - Current Expenditures of Individual Debtor(s)	Yes	1			3,034.
Total Number of Sheets of ALL Schedules		17			
Total Assets			20,032.00		
Total Liabilities				74,905.00	

n re   **Robert John Doe,**
      Dora Jean Doe

Case No. _____

_____,
                 Debtors

SCHEDULE A. REAL PROPERTY

Except as directed below, list all real property in which the debtor has any legal, equitable, or future interest, including all property owned as a enant, community property, or in which the debtor has a life estate. Include any property in which the debtor holds rights and powers exercisable for debtor's own benefit. If the debtor is married, state whether husband, wife, or both own the property by placing an "H," "W," "J," or "C" in the column eled "Husband, Wife, Joint, or Community." If the debtor holds no interest in real property, write "None" under "Description and Location of Property."

Do not include interests in executory contracts and unexpired leases on this schedule. List them in Schedule G - Executory Contracts and Unexpired ases.

If an entity claims to have a lien or hold a secured interest in any property, state the amount of the secured claim. (See Schedule D.) If no entity ims to hold a secured interest in the property, write "None" in the column labeled "Amount of Secured Claim."

If the debtor is an individual or if a joint petition is filed, state the amount of any exemption claimed in the property only in Schedule C - Property imed as Exempt.

Description and Location of Property	Nature of Debtor's Interest in Property	Husband, Wife, Joint, or Community	Current Market Value of Debtor's Interest in Property, without Deducting any Secured Claim or Exemption	Amount of Secured Claim
None				

	Sub-Total >	**0.00**	(Total of this page)
	Total >	**0.00**	

0   continuation sheets attached to the Schedule of Real Property

(Report also on Summary of Schedules)

In re **Robert John Doe,** Case No. _____
    Dora Jean Doe

_____ ,
                    Debtors

SCHEDULE B. PERSONAL PROPERTY

Except as directed below, list all personal property of the debtor of whatever kind. If the debtor has no property in one or more of the categories, pl
an "x" in the appropriate position in the column labeled "None." If additional space is needed in any category, attach a separate sheet properly identi
with the case name, case number, and the number of the category. If the debtor is married, state whether husband, wife, or both own the property by plac
an "H," "W," "J," or "C" in the column labeled "Husband, Wife, Joint, or Community." If the debtor is an individual or a joint petition is filed, state
amount of any exemptions claimed only in Schedule C - Property Claimed as Exempt.

Do not list interests in executory contracts and unexpired leases on this schedule. List them in Schedule G - Executory Contracts and Unexpired Lea

If the property is being held for the debtor by someone else, state that person's name and address under "Description and Location of Property."

Type of Property	N O N E	Description and Location of Property	Husband, Wife, Joint, or Community	Current Market Value o Debtor's Interest in Prope without Deducting any Secured Claim or Exempt
1. Cash on hand		Cash on hand - in debtor's possession	H	60.00
		Cash on hand - in debtor's possession	W	30.00
2. Checking, savings or other financial accounts, certificates of deposit, or shares in banks, savings and loan, thrift, building and loan, and homestead associations, or credit unions, brokerage houses, or cooperatives.		Checking account with number ending in 7842 at Fairfax Bank (237); Savings account with number ending in 0276 at Fairfax Bank (402)	J	639.00
3. Security deposits with public utilities, telephone companies, landlords, and others.		Security deposit with Happy Apartments, 426 Happy Lane, Fairfax VA 22034	J	900.00
4. Household goods and furnishings, including audio, video, and computer equipment.		TV (100); Stereo (325); VCR (40); DVD player (50); Sofa (100); Love seat (50); Tables (100); Lamps (35); Dining room table and chairs (450); Buffet (75); Book shelves (100); Beds and bedding (375); Home computer (100); Microwave oven (35); Kitchen appliances (50); Dishes (20); Miscellaneous household goods (100) - in debtors' home	J	2,105.00
5. Books, pictures and other art objects, antiques, stamp, coin, record, tape, compact disc, and other collections or collectibles.		Books (200); Pictures (50); Salt and pepper shaker collection (100) - in debtors' home	J	350.00
6. Wearing apparel.		Clothes	H	100.00
		Clothes	W	250.00
7. Furs and jewelry.		Wedding ring - in debtor's possession	H	50.00
		Wedding ring (200); engagement ring (450) - in debtor's possession	W	650.00

Sub-Total > **5,134.00**
(Total of this page)

__3__ continuation sheets attached to the Schedule of Personal Property

Case No. _____

_____ ,
Debtors

SCHEDULE B. PERSONAL PROPERTY
(Continuation Sheet)

Type of Property	N O N E	Description and Location of Property	Husband, Wife, Joint, or Community	Current Market Value of Debtor's Interest in Property, without Deducting any Secured Claim or Exemption
Firearms and sports, photographic, and other hobby equipment.		**Digital camera - in debtor's possession**	**H**	**100.00**
		Mountain bike - in debtor's possession	**W**	**100.00**
Interests in insurance policies. Name insurance company of each policy and itemize surrender or refund value of each.		**Interest in whole-life policy with Secured Investment Life Insurance Company**	**H**	**2,173.00**
Annuities. Itemize and name each issuer.	X			
Interests in IRA, ERISA, Keogh, or other pension or profit sharing plans. Itemize.		**401 K account with Middle Kingdom Software Company - not property of the estate**	**H**	**975.00**
Stock and interests in incorporated and unincorporated businesses. Itemize.	X			
Interests in partnerships or joint ventures. Itemize.	X			
Government and corporate bonds and other negotiable and nonnegotiable instruments.	X			
Accounts receivable.	X			
Alimony, maintenance, support, and property settlements to which the debtor is or may be entitled. Give particulars.	X			
Other liquidated debts owing debtor including tax refunds. Give particulars.	X	**2005 federal tax refund**	**J**	**890.00**
Equitable or future interests, life estates, and rights or powers exercisable for the benefit of the debtor other than those listed in Schedule of Real Property.	X			

	Sub-Total > (Total of this page)	**4,238.00**

Sheet __1__ of __3__ continuation sheets attached
to the Schedule of Personal Property

SCHEDULE B. PERSONAL PROPERTY
(Continuation Sheet)

Type of Property	N O N E	Description and Location of Property	Husband, Wife, Joint, or Community	Current Market Value of Debtor's Interest in Property without Deducting any Secured Claim or Exempt
19. Contingent and noncontingent interests in estate of a decedent, death benefit plan, life insurance policy, or trust.	X			
20. Other contingent and unliquidated claims of every nature, including tax refunds, counterclaims of the debtor, and rights to setoff claims. Give estimated value of each.	X			
21. Patents, copyrights, and other intellectual property. Give particulars.	X			
22. Licenses, franchises, and other general intangibles. Give particulars.	X			
23. Automobiles, trucks, trailers, and other vehicles and accessories.		2003 Honda Civic - good condition, 37,800 miles - in debtors' possession	J	9,760.00
		1999 Ford Escort - fair condition, 127,000 miles - in debtors' possession	J	900.00
24. Boats, motors, and accessories.	X			
25. Aircraft and accessories.	X			
26. Office equipment, furnishings, and supplies.	X			
27. Machinery, fixtures, equipment, and supplies used in business.	X			
28. Inventory.	X			
29. Animals.	X			
30. Crops - growing or harvested. Give particulars.	X			
31. Farming equipment and implements.	X			

Sub-Total >   **10,660.00**
(Total of this page)

Sheet __**2**__ of __**3**__ continuation sheets attached
to the Schedule of Personal Property

Best Case Bankruptcy

_____,
Debtors

SCHEDULE B. PERSONAL PROPERTY
(Continuation Sheet)

Type of Property	N O N E	Description and Location of Property	Husband, Wife, Joint, or Community	Current Market Value of Debtor's Interest in Property, without Deducting any Secured Claim or Exemption
. Farm supplies, chemicals, and feed.	**X**			
. Other personal property of any kind not already listed.				

	Sub-Total > (Total of this page)	
	Total >	**20,032.00**

(Report also on Summary of Schedules)

In re **Robert John Doe,**
       Dora Jean Doe

Case No. _____

_____,
Debtors

SCHEDULE C. PROPERTY CLAIMED AS EXEMPT

Debtor elects the exemptions to which debtor is entitled under:

[Check one box]

☐ 11 U.S.C. §522(b)(1): Exemptions provided in 11 U.S.C. §522(d). Note: These exemptions are available only in certain states.

■ 11 U.S.C. §522(b)(2): Exemptions available under applicable nonbankruptcy federal laws, state or local law where the debtor's domicile has been located for the 180 days immediately preceding the filing of the petition, or for a longer portion of the 180-day period than in any other place, and the debtor's interest as a tenant by the entirety or joint tenant to the extent the interest is exempt from process under applicable nonbankruptcy law.

Description of Property	Specify Law Providing Each Exemption	Value of Claimed Exemption	Current Market Value Property Without Deducting Exemption
Cash on Hand			
Cash on hand - in debtor's possession	Va. Code Ann. § 34-4	60.00	60.00
Cash on hand - in debtor's possession	Va. Code Ann. § 34-4	30.00	30.00
Checking, Savings, or Other Financial Accounts, Certificates of Deposit			
Checking account with number ending in 7842 at Fairfax Bank (237); Savings account with number ending in 0276 at Fairfax Bank (402)	Va. Code Ann. § 34-4	639.00	639.00
Security Deposits with Utilities, Landlords, and Others			
Security deposit with Happy Apartments, 426 Happy Lane, Fairfax VA 22034	Va. Code Ann. § 34-4	900.00	900.00
Household Goods and Furnishings			
TV (100); Stereo (325); VCR (40); DVD player (50); Sofa (100); Love seat (50); Tables (100); Lamps (35); Dining room table and chairs (450); Buffet (75); Book shelves (100); Beds and bedding (375); Home computer (100); Microwave oven (35); Kitchen appliances (50); Dishes (20); Miscellaneous household goods (100) - in debtors' home	Va. Code Ann. § 34-26(4a)	2,105.00	2,105.00
Books, Pictures and Other Art Objects; Collectibles			
Books (200); Pictures (50); Salt and pepper shaker collection (100) - in debtors' home	Va. Code Ann. § 34-4	350.00	350.00
Wearing Apparel			
Clothes	Va. Code Ann. § 34-26(4)	100.00	100.00
Clothes	Va. Code Ann. § 34-26(4)	250.00	250.00
Furs and Jewelry			
Wedding ring - in debtor's possession	Va. Code Ann. § 34-26(1a)	50.00	50.00
Wedding ring (200); engagement ring (450) - in debtor's possession	Va. Code Ann. § 34-26(1a)	650.00	650.00
Firearms and Sports, Photographic and Other Hobby Equipment			
Digital camera - in debtor's possession	Va. Code Ann. § 34-4	100.00	100.00
Mountain bike - in debtor's possession	Va. Code Ann. § 34-4	100.00	100.00
Interests in Insurance Policies			
Interest in whole-life policy with Secured Investment Life Insurance Company	Va. Code Ann. § 34-4	2,173.00	2,173.00

___1___ continuation sheets attached to Schedule of Property Claimed as Exempt

In re   **Robert John Doe,**
         Dora Jean Doe

Case No. _____

_____,
            Debtors

SCHEDULE C. PROPERTY CLAIMED AS EXEMPT
(Continuation Sheet)

Description of Property	Specify Law Providing Each Exemption	Value of Claimed Exemption	Current Market Value of Property Without Deducting Exemption
Interests in IRA, ERISA, Keogh, or Other Pension or Profit Sharing Plans			
401K account with Middle Kingdom Software Company - not property of the estate	29 U.S.C.A. § 1056(d)	975.00	975.00
Automobiles, Trucks, Trailers, and Other Vehicles			
1989 Ford Escort - fair condition, 127,000 miles in debtors' possession	Va. Code Ann. § 34-26(8)	900.00	900.00
Other Liquidated Debts Owing Debtor			
1995 federal tax refund	Va. Code Ann. § 34-4	890.00	890.00

Sheet ___**1**___ of ___**1**___ continuation sheets attached to the Schedule of Property Claimed as Exempt

Best Case Bankruptcy

Form B6D
(12/03)

In re   **Robert John Doe,**
      Dora Jean Doe

Case No. _____

_____ ,
                           Debtors

SCHEDULE D. CREDITORS HOLDING SECURED CLAIMS

State the name, mailing address, including zip code and last four digits of any account number of all entities holding claims secured by property of the debtor as of the date of filing of the petition. The complete account number of any account the debtor has with the creditor is useful to the trustee and the creditor and may be provided if the debtor chooses to do so. List creditors holding all types of secured interests such as judgment liens, garnishments, statutory liens, mortgages, deeds of trust, and other security interests. List creditors in alphabetical order to the extent practicable. If all secured creditors will not fit on this page, use the continuation sheet provided.

If any entity other than a spouse in a joint case may be jointly liable on a claim, place an "X" in the column labeled "Codebtor", include the entity on the appropriate schedule of creditors, and complete Schedule H - Codebtors. If a joint petition is filed, state whether husband, wife, both of them, or the marital community may be liable on each claim by placing an "H", "W", "J", or "C" in the column labeled "Husband, Wife, Joint, or Community."

If the claim is contingent, place an "X" in the column labeled "Contingent". If the claim is unliquidated, place an "X" in the column labeled "Unliquidated". If the claim is disputed, place an "X" in the column labeled "Disputed". (You may need to place an "X" in more than one of these three columns.)

Report the total of all claims listed on this schedule in the box labeled "Total" on the last sheet of the completed schedule. Report this total also on the Summary of Schedules.

☐   Check this box if debtor has no creditors holding secured claims to report on this Schedule D.

CREDITOR'S NAME, AND MAILING ADDRESS INCLUDING ZIP CODE, AND ACCOUNT NUMBER (See instructions above.)	CODEBTOR	Husband, Wife, Joint, or Community		DATE CLAIM WAS INCURRED, NATURE OF LIEN, AND DESCRIPTION AND MARKET VALUE OF PROPERTY SUBJECT TO LIEN	CONTINGENT	UNLIQUIDATED	DISPUTED	AMOUNT OF CLAIM WITHOUT DEDUCTING VALUE OF COLLATERAL	UNSECURED PORTION IF ANY
		H W	J C						
Account No. **xx-xxx-9547** **Honda Finance Corp.** **121 Continental Drive** **Newark, DE 19713**		J		**1/03** **Purchase Money Security** **2003 Honda Civic - good condition, 37,800 miles - in debtors' possession** Value $ **9,760.00**				**14,089.00**	**4,329.0**
Account No. Value $									
Account No. Value $									
Account No. Value $									

  0   continuation sheets attached

	Subtotal (Total of this page)	**14,089.00**
	Total (Report on Summary of Schedules)	**14,089.00**

In re __Robert John Doe,__   Case No. _____

       __Dora Jean Doe__

_____,

Debtors

SCHEDULE E. CREDITORS HOLDING UNSECURED PRIORITY CLAIMS

A complete list of claims entitled to priority, listed separately by type of priority, is to be set forth on the sheets provided. Only holders of unsecured claims entitled to priority should be listed in this schedule. In the boxes provided on the attached sheets, state the name, mailing address, including zip code, and last four digits of the account number, if any, of all entities holding priority claims against the debtor or the property of the debtor, as of the date of the filing of the petition. The complete account number of any account the debtor has with the creditor is useful to the trustee and the creditor and may be provided if the debtor chooses to do so.

If any entity other than a spouse in a joint case may be jointly liable on a claim, place an "X" in the column labeled "Codebtor", include the entity on the appropriate schedule of creditors, and complete Schedule H-Codebtors. If a joint petition is filed, state whether husband, wife, both of them or the marital community may be liable on each claim by placing an "H", "W", "J", or "C" in the column labeled "Husband, Wife, Joint, or Community".

If the claim is contingent, place an "X" in the column labeled "Contingent". If the claim is unliquidated, place an "X" in the column labeled "Unliquidated". If the claim is disputed, place an "X" in the column labeled "Disputed". (You may need to place an "X" in more than one of these three columns.)

Report the total of claims listed on each sheet in the box labeled "Subtotal" on each sheet. Report the total of all claims listed on this Schedule E in the box labeled "Total" on the last sheet of the completed schedule. Repeat this total also on the Summary of Schedules.

☐ Check this box if debtor has no creditors holding unsecured priority claims to report on this Schedule E.

TYPES OF PRIORITY CLAIMS (Check the appropriate box(es) below if claims in that category are listed on the attached sheets.)

☐ **Extensions of credit in an involuntary case**

    Claims arising in the ordinary course of the debtor's business or financial affairs after the commencement of the case but before the earlier of the appointment of a trustee or the order for relief. 11 U.S.C. § 507(a)(2).

☐ **Wages, salaries, and commissions**

    Wages, salaries, and commissions, including vacation, severance, and sick leave pay owing to employees and commissions owing to qualifying independent sales representatives up to $4,650* per person earned within 90 days immediately preceding the filing of the original petition, or the cessation of business, which ever occurred first, to the extent provided in 11 U.S.C. § 507 (a)(3).

☐ **Contributions to employee benefit plans**

    Money owed to employee benefit plans for services rendered within 180 days immediately preceding the filing of the original petition, or the cessation of business, whichever occurred first, to the extent provided in 11 U.S.C. § 507(a)(4).

☐ **Certain farmers and fishermen**

    Claims of certain farmers and fishermen, up to $4,650* per farmer or fisherman, against the debtor, as provided in 11 U.S.C. § 507(a)(5).

☐ **Deposits by individuals**

    Claims of individuals up to $2,100* for deposits for the purchase, lease, or rental of property or services for personal, family, or household use, that were not delivered or provided. 11 U.S.C. § 507(a)(6).

☐ **Alimony, Maintenance, or Support**

    Claims of a spouse, former spouse, or child of the debtor for alimony, maintenance, or support, to the extent provided in 11 U.S.C. § 507(a)(7).

■ **Taxes and Certain Other Debts Owed to Governmental Units**

    Taxes, customs duties, and penalties owing to federal, state, and local governmental units as set forth in 11 U.S.C § 507(a)(8).

☐ **Commitments to Maintain the Capital of an Insured Depository Institution**

    Claims based on commitments to the FDIC, RTC, Director of the Office of Thrift Supervision, Comptroller of the Currency, or Board of Governors of the Federal Reserve System, or their predecessors or successors, to maintain the capital of an insured depository institution. 11 U.S.C. § 507(a)(9).

*Amounts are subject to adjustment on April 1, 2004, and every three years thereafter with respect to cases commenced on or after the date of adjustment.

                  __1__ continuation sheets attached

In re   **Robert John Doe,**
        Dora Jean Doe

Case No. _____

_____,
                 Debtors

SCHEDULE E. CREDITORS HOLDING UNSECURED PRIORITY CLAIMS
(Continuation Sheet)

**Taxes and Certain Other Debts
Owed to Governmental Units**

TYPE OF PRIORITY

| CREDITOR'S NAME, AND MAILING ADDRESS INCLUDING ZIP CODE, AND ACCOUNT NUMBER (See instructions.) | C O D E B T O R | Husband, Wife, Joint, or Community | | C O N T I N G E N T | U N L I Q U I D A T E D | D I S P U T E D | TOTAL AMOUNT OF CLAIM | AMOUNT ENTITLED TO PRIORITY |
		H W J C	DATE CLAIM WAS INCURRED AND CONSIDERATION FOR CLAIM					
Account No. **xxx-xx-6789** **VA Dept. of Taxation** **Legal Unit - Office Svc. Div.** **PO Box 6-L** **Richmond, VA 23282**	J		**5/1/05** **2004 state income tax**				**578.00**	**578.0**
Account No.								
Account No.								
Account No.								
Account No.								

Sheet __1__ of __1__ continuation sheets attached to
Schedule of Creditors Holding Unsecured Priority Claims

Subtotal (Total of this page)	**578.00**
Total (Report on Summary of Schedules)	**578.00**

n re   **Robert John Doe,**
        Dora Jean Doe   Case No. _____

_____ ,
                                                    Debtors

SCHEDULE F. CREDITORS HOLDING UNSECURED NONPRIORITY CLAIMS

State the name, mailing address, including zip code, and last four digits of any account number, of all entities holding unsecured claims without
ority against the debtor or the property of the debtor, as of the date of filing of the petition. The complete account number of any account the debtor
s with the creditor is useful to the trustee and the creditor and may be provided if the debtor chooses to do so. Do not include claims listed in
hedules D and E. If all creditors will not fit on this page, use the continuation sheet provided.

If any entity other than a spouse in a joint case may be jointly liable on a claim, place an "X" in the column labeled "Codebtor", include the entity
the appropriate schedule of creditors, and complete Schedule H - Codebtors. If a joint petition is filed, state whether husband, wife, both of them, or
marital community maybe liable on each claim by placing an "H", "W", "J", or "C" in the column labeled "Husband, Wife, Joint, or Community".

If the claim is contingent, place an "X" in the column labeled "Contingent". If the claim is unliquidated, place an "X" in the column labeled
nliquidated". If the claim is disputed, place an "X" in the column labeled "Disputed". (You may need to place an "X" in more than one of these three
lumns.)

Report the total of all claims listed on this schedule in the box labeled "Total" on the last sheet of the completed schedule. Report this total also on
e Summary of Schedules.

☐ Check this box if debtor has no creditors holding unsecured claims to report on this Schedule F.

CREDITOR'S NAME, AND MAILING ADDRESS INCLUDING ZIP CODE, AND ACCOUNT NUMBER (See instructions above.)	C O D E B T O R	Husband, Wife, Joint, or Community		DATE CLAIM WAS INCURRED AND CONSIDERATION FOR CLAIM. IF CLAIM IS SUBJECT TO SETOFF, SO STATE.	C O N T I N G E N T	U N L I Q U I D A T E D	D I S P U T E D	AMOUNT OF CLAIM
		H W	J C					
ount No. **xxxxxxxx9567** erican Express General Warren Blvd. vern, PA 19355			J	6/97 - 8/04 **Credit card purchases**				8,456.00
ount No. **xxxxxxxxxx6666** ly Total Fitness Corp. Box 42006 timore, MD 21284-2006		H		7/03 **Health club membership**				470.00
ount No. **xxxxxxxxx2422** ital One Box 26074 hmond, VA 23260			J	6/01 - 8/04 **Credit card purchases**				10,237.00
ount No. **35645234233210** umbia House Box 1114 re Haute, IN 47811-1114		W		7/98 - 2/04 **Merchandise**			X	17.00
___ continuation sheets attached				Subtotal (Total of this page)				19,180.00

S/N:20657-031103   Best Case Bankruptcy

In re   **Robert John Doe,**   Case No. _____

         Dora Jean Doe

                                                 Debtors

SCHEDULE F. CREDITORS HOLDING UNSECURED NONPRIORITY CLAIMS
(Continuation Sheet)

CREDITOR'S NAME, AND MAILING ADDRESS INCLUDING ZIP CODE, AND ACCOUNT NUMBER (See instructions.)	CODEBTOR	Husband, Wife, Joint, or Community				DATE CLAIM WAS INCURRED AND CONSIDERATION FOR CLAIM. IF CLAIM IS SUBJECT TO SETOFF, SO STATE.	CONTINGENT	UNLIQUIDATED	DISPUTED	AMOUNT OF CLAIM
		H	W	J	C					
Account No. **PRF782** **Dr. George Smith** **8742 Doctors Lane** **Arlington, VA 22207**			W			8/03 **Medical service**				820
Account No. **xxxxx4334** **Fair Oaks Hospital** **PO Box 16010** **Falls Church, VA 22040-1610**			W			8/7/03 **Medical service**				12,076
Account No. **xxxxxxxxxxxxxx5344** **MBNA** **Asset Acceptance Corp.** **PO Box 318035** **Independence, OH 44131**			W			4/01 - 9/03 **Credit card purchases**				9,321
Account No. **xxxxxxxxx6922** **Mobil Oil/MCFC** **PO Box 85061** **Tulsa, OK 74121-2001**				J		7/02 - 4/03 **Credit card purchases**				320
Account No. **xxxxx-6789** **Sallie Mae Servicing** **PO Box 9500** **Wilkes-Barre, PA 18773-9500**		H				7/99 **Student loan**				12,789

Sheet no. __**1**__ of _**2**__ sheets attached to Schedule of   Subtotal
Creditors Holding Unsecured Nonpriority Claims   (Total of this page)   **35,326**

In re   **Robert John Doe,**   Case No. _____
         Dora Jean Doe

                                       Debtors

SCHEDULE F. CREDITORS HOLDING UNSECURED NONPRIORITY CLAIMS
(Continuation Sheet)

CREDITOR'S NAME, AND MAILING ADDRESS INCLUDING ZIP CODE, AND ACCOUNT NUMBER (See instructions.)	CODEBTOR	Husband, Wife, Joint, or Community				DATE CLAIM WAS INCURRED AND CONSIDERATION FOR CLAIM. IF CLAIM IS SUBJECT TO SETOFF, SO STATE.	CONTINGENT	UNLIQUIDATED	DISPUTED	AMOUNT OF CLAIM
		H	W	J	C					
count No. **xxxxxxxxxx3232**						3/89 - 10/03 **Credit card purchases**				
ars Box 818017 veland, OH 44181-8017				J						
										5,732.00
count No.										
count No.										
count No.										
count No.										

eet no. **2** of **2** sheets attached to Schedule of
editors Holding Unsecured Nonpriority Claims

Subtotal (Total of this page)	5,732.00
Total (Report on Summary of Schedules)	60,238.00

In re   **Robert John Doe,**
        Dora Jean Doe
                                           Case No._____

                                     Debtors

SCHEDULE G. EXECUTORY CONTRACTS AND UNEXPIRED LEASES

Describe all executory contracts of any nature and all unexpired leases of real or personal property. Include any timeshare interests.
State nature of debtor's interest in contract, i.e., "Purchaser," "Agent," etc. State whether debtor is the lessor or lessee of a lease.
Provide the names and complete mailing addresses of all other parties to each lease or contract described.

NOTE: A party listed on this schedule will not receive notice of the filing of this case unless the party is also scheduled in the appropriate
           schedule of creditors.

☐ Check this box if debtor has no executory contracts or unexpired leases.

Name and Mailing Address, Including Zip Code, of Other Parties to Lease or Contract	Description of Contract or Lease and Nature of Debtor's Interest. State whether lease is for nonresidential real property. State contract number of any government contract.
Happy Apartments **426 Happy Lane** **Fairfax, VA 22034**	**lease for apartment - expires 9/05 - debtors will** **maintain**

  0   continuation sheets attached to Schedule of Executory Contracts and Unexpired Leases

In re   **Robert John Doe,**   Case No. _____
         Dora Jean Doe

_____ ,
                               Debtors

SCHEDULE H. CODEBTORS

Provide the information requested concerning any person or entity, other than a spouse in a joint case, that is also liable on any debts listed by debtor in the schedules of creditors. Include all guarantors and co-signers. In community property states, a married debtor not filing a joint case should report the name and address of the nondebtor spouse on this schedule. Include all names used by the nondebtor spouse during the six years immediately preceding the commencement of this case.

■ Check this box if debtor has no codebtors.

NAME AND ADDRESS OF CODEBTOR	NAME AND ADDRESS OF CREDITOR

0   continuation sheets attached to Schedule of Codebtors

In re   **Robert John Doe,**   Case No. _____
             Dora Jean Doe

                                    Debtors

SCHEDULE I. CURRENT INCOME OF INDIVIDUAL DEBTOR(S)

The column labeled "Spouse" must be completed in all cases filed by joint debtors and by a married debtor in a chapter 12 or 13 case whether or not a joint petition is filed, unless the spouses are separated and a joint petition is not filed.

Debtor's Marital Status:	DEPENDENTS OF DEBTOR AND SPOUSE	
	RELATIONSHIP	AGE
Married	**Daughter** **Son** **Daughter**	**3 years** **5 years** **8 years**

EMPLOYMENT:	DEBTOR	SPOUSE
Occupation	**computer specialist**	**security officer**
Name of Employer	**Middle Kingdom Software Company**	**Security Inc.**
How long employed	**six months**	**one year**
Address of Employer	**948 Dotcom Blvd.** **Alexandria, VA 22314**	**5672 Industrial Park Lane** **Falls Church, VA 22042**

INCOME: (Estimate of average monthly income)	DEBTOR	SPOUSE
Current monthly gross wages, salary, and commissions (pro rate if not paid monthly)	$ **3,583.82**	$ **1,157.00**
Estimated monthly overtime	$ **0.00**	$ **0.00**
SUBTOTAL	$ **3,583.82**	$ **1,157.00**
LESS PAYROLL DEDUCTIONS		
a. Payroll taxes and social security	$ **996.50**	$ **324.5?**
b. Insurance	$ **379.17**	$ **0.00**
c. Union dues	$ **0.00**	$ **0.00**
d. Other (Specify) **401 K deduction**	$ **162.50**	$ **0.00**
charity	$ **0.00**	$ **21.6**
SUBTOTAL OF PAYROLL DEDUCTIONS	$ **1,538.17**	$ **346.2?**
TOTAL NET MONTHLY TAKE HOME PAY	$ **2,045.65**	$ **810.7?**
Regular income from operation of business or profession or farm (attach detailed statement)	$ **0.00**	$ **0.00**
Income from real property	$ **0.00**	$ **0.00**
Interest and dividends	$ **0.00**	$ **0.00**
Alimony, maintenance or support payments payable to the debtor for the debtor's use or that of dependents listed above	$ **0.00**	$ **0.00**
Social security or other government assistance (Specify) _____	$ **0.00**	$ **0.00**
_____	$ **0.00**	$ **0.00**
Pension or retirement income	$ **0.00**	$ **0.00**
Other monthly income (Specify) _____	$ **0.00**	$ **0.00**
_____	$ **0.00**	$ **0.00**
TOTAL MONTHLY INCOME	$ **2,045.65**	$ **810.7?**

TOTAL COMBINED MONTHLY INCOME $ ____**2,856.40**____   (Report also on Summary of Schedules)

Describe any increase or decrease of more than 10% in any of the above categories anticipated to occur within the year following the filing of this document:

SCHEDULE J. CURRENT EXPENDITURES OF INDIVIDUAL DEBTOR(S)

Complete this schedule by estimating the average monthly expenses of the debtor and the debtor's family. Pro rate any payments made bi-weekly, quarterly, semi-annually, or annually to show monthly rate.

☐ Check this box if a joint petition is filed and debtor's spouse maintains a separate household. Complete a separate schedule of expenditures labeled "Spouse."

Rent or home mortgage payment (include lot rented for mobile home)	$	950.00
Are real estate taxes included? Yes_____ No___X___		
Is property insurance included? Yes_____ No___X___		
Utilities: Electricity and heating fuel	$	125.00
Water and sewer	$	0.00
Telephone	$	40.00
Other_____	$	0.00
Home maintenance (repairs and upkeep)	$	10.00
Food	$	600.00
Clothing	$	100.00
Laundry and dry cleaning	$	20.00
Medical and dental expenses	$	60.00
Transportation (not including car payments)	$	180.00
Recreation, clubs and entertainment, newspapers, magazines, etc.	$	20.00
Charitable contributions	$	55.00
Insurance (not deducted from wages or included in home mortgage payments)		
Homeowner's or renter's	$	20.00
Life	$	30.00
Health	$	0.00
Auto	$	80.00
Other_____	$	0.00
Taxes (not deducted from wages or included in home mortgage payments)		
(Specify)_____	$	0.00
Installment payments: (In chapter 12 and 13 cases, do not list payments to be included in the plan.)		
Auto	$	224.00
Other___**student loan**_____	$	80.00
Other_____	$	0.00
Other_____	$	0.00
Alimony, maintenance, and support paid to others	$	0.00
Payments for support of additional dependents not living at your home	$	0.00
Regular expenses from operation of business, profession, or farm (attach detailed statement)	$	0.00
Other_____**day care (320); hair cuts (40)**_____	$	360.00
Other_____**Misc. household expenses**_____	$	80.00
TOTAL MONTHLY EXPENSES (Report also on Summary of Schedules)	$	3,034.00

[FOR CHAPTER 12 AND 13 DEBTORS ONLY]

Provide the information requested below, including whether plan payments are to be made bi-weekly, monthly, annually, or at some other regular interval.

A. Total projected monthly income	$	N/A
B. Total projected monthly expenses	$	N/A
C. Excess income (A minus B)	$	N/A
D. Total amount to be paid into plan each _____	$	N/A

(interval)

United States Bankruptcy Court
Eastern District of Virginia

In re   **Robert John Doe**
      Dora Jean Doe
                   Debtor(s)

Case No. _____

Chapter   **7**   _____

DECLARATION CONCERNING DEBTOR'S SCHEDULES

DECLARATION UNDER PENALTY OF PERJURY BY INDIVIDUAL DEBTOR

      I declare under penalty of perjury that I have read the foregoing summary and schedules, consisting of __**18**__ sheets *[total shown on summary page plus 1]*, and that they are true and correct to the best of my knowledge, information, and belief.

Date   **December 10, 2004**   Signature _____

                                           Robert John Doe
                                           Debtor

Date   **December 10, 2004**   Signature _____

                                           Dora Jean Doe
                                           Joint Debtor

Penalty for making a false statement or concealing property: Fine of up to $500,000 or imprisonment for up to 5 years or both.
18 U.S.C. §§ 152 and 3571.

United States Bankruptcy Court
Eastern District of Virginia

In re   **Robert John Doe**
    Dora Jean Doe   Case No. _____

                                                 Debtor(s)   Chapter   **7** _____

STATEMENT OF FINANCIAL AFFAIRS

This statement is to be completed by every debtor. Spouses filing a joint petition may file a single statement on which the information for both spouses is combined. If the case is filed under chapter 12 or chapter 13, a married debtor must furnish information for both spouses whether or not a joint petition is filed, unless the spouses are separated and a joint petition is not filed. An individual debtor engaged in business as a sole proprietor, partner, family farmer, or self-employed professional, should provide the information requested on this statement concerning all such activities as well as the individual's personal affairs.

Questions 1 - 18 are to be completed by all debtors. Debtors that are or have been in business, as defined below, also must complete Questions 19 - 25. **If the answer to an applicable question is "None," mark the box labeled "None."** If additional space is needed for the answer to any question, use and attach a separate sheet properly identified with the case name, case number (if known), and the number of the question.

DEFINITIONS

"In business." A debtor is "in business" for the purpose of this form if the debtor is a corporation or partnership. An individual debtor is "in business" for the purpose of this form if the debtor is or has been, within the six years immediately preceding the filing of this bankruptcy case, any of the following: an officer, director, managing executive, or owner of 5 percent or more of the voting or equity securities of a corporation; a partner, other than a limited partner, of a partnership; a sole proprietor or self-employed.

"Insider." The term "insider" includes but is not limited to: relatives of the debtor; general partners of the debtor and their relatives; corporations of which the debtor is an officer, director, or person in control; officers, directors, and any owner of 5 percent or more of the voting or equity securities of a corporate debtor and their relatives; affiliates of the debtor and insiders of such affiliates; any managing agent of the debtor. 11 U.S.C. § 101.

---

1. Income from employment or operation of business

None
☐

State the gross amount of income the debtor has received from employment, trade, or profession, or from operation of the debtor's business from the beginning of this calendar year to the date this case was commenced. State also the gross amounts received during the **two years** immediately preceding this calendar year. (A debtor that maintains, or has maintained, financial records on the basis of a fiscal rather than a calendar year may report fiscal year income. Identify the beginning and ending dates of the debtor's fiscal year.) If a joint petition is filed, state income for each spouse separately. (Married debtors filing under chapter 12 or chapter 13 must state income of both spouses whether or not a joint petition is filed, unless the spouses are separated and a joint petition is not filed.)

AMOUNT	SOURCE (if more than one)
$16,250.00	**Employment for husband in 2005**
$9,256.00	**Employment for wife in 2005**
$11,230.00	**Employment for husband in 2004**
$7,843.00	**Employment for wife in 2004**
$58,000.00	**Employment for husband in 2003**

2. Income other than from employment or operation of business

None
■

State the amount of income received by the debtor other than from employment, trade, profession, or operation of the debtor's business during the **two years** immediately preceding the commencement of this case. Give particulars. If a joint petition is filed, state income for each spouse separately. (Married debtors filing under chapter 12 or chapter 13 must state income for each spouse whether or not a joint petition is filed, unless the spouses are separated and a joint petition is not filed.)

AMOUNT	SOURCE

3. Payments to creditors

None
☐

a. List all payments on loans, installment purchases of goods or services, and other debts, aggregating more than $600 to any creditor, made within **90 days** immediately preceding the commencement of this case. (Married debtors filing under chapter 12 or chapter 13 must include payments by either or both spouses whether or not a joint petition is filed, unless the spouses are separated and a joint petition is not filed.)

NAME AND ADDRESS OF CREDITOR	DATES OF PAYMENTS	AMOUNT PAID	AMOUNT STILL OWING
Honda Finance Corp. **121 Continental Drive** **Newark, DE 19713**	**2/5/05; 3/7/05; 4/2/05**	**$981.00**	**$14,089.00**

None
■

b. List all payments made within **one year** immediately preceding the commencement of this case to or for the benefit of creditors who are or were insiders. (Married debtors filing under chapter 12 or chapter 13 must include payments by either or both spouses whether or not a joint petition is filed, unless the spouses are separated and a joint petition is not filed.)

NAME AND ADDRESS OF CREDITOR AND RELATIONSHIP TO DEBTOR	DATE OF PAYMENT	AMOUNT PAID	AMOUNT STILL OWING

4. Suits and administrative proceedings, executions, garnishments and attachments

None
☐

a. List all suits and administrative proceedings to which the debtor is or was a party within **one year** immediately preceding the filing of this bankruptcy case. (Married debtors filing under chapter 12 or chapter 13 must include information concerning either or both spouses whether or not a joint petition is filed, unless the spouses are separated and a joint petition is not filed.)

CAPTION OF SUIT AND CASE NUMBER	NATURE OF PROCEEDING	COURT OR AGENCY AND LOCATION	STATUS OR DISPOSITION
Capitol One v. Robert and Dora Doe **Case No. 05-17634**	**Warrant in debt**	**General District Court of Fairfax County**	**pending**

None
■

b. Describe all property that has been attached, garnished or seized under any legal or equitable process within **one year** immediately preceding the commencement of this case. (Married debtors filing under chapter 12 or chapter 13 must include information concerning property of either or both spouses whether or not a joint petition is filed, unless the spouses are separated and a joint petition is not filed.)

NAME AND ADDRESS OF PERSON FOR WHOSE BENEFIT PROPERTY WAS SEIZED	DATE OF SEIZURE	DESCRIPTION AND VALUE OF PROPERTY

5. Repossessions, foreclosures and returns

None
■

List all property that has been repossessed by a creditor, sold at a foreclosure sale, transferred through a deed in lieu of foreclosure or returned to the seller, within **one year** immediately preceding the commencement of this case. (Married debtors filing under chapter 12 or chapter 13 must include information concerning property of either or both spouses whether or not a joint petition is filed, unless the spouses are separated and a joint petition is not filed.)

NAME AND ADDRESS OF CREDITOR OR SELLER	DATE OF REPOSSESSION, FORECLOSURE SALE, TRANSFER OR RETURN	DESCRIPTION AND VALUE OF PROPERTY

6. Assignments and receiverships

None ■   a. Describe any assignment of property for the benefit of creditors made within **120 days** immediately preceding the commencement of this case. (Married debtors filing under chapter 12 or chapter 13 must include any assignment by either or both spouses whether or not a joint petition is filed, unless the spouses are separated and a joint petition is not filed.)

NAME AND ADDRESS OF ASSIGNEE	DATE OF ASSIGNMENT	TERMS OF ASSIGNMENT OR SETTLEMENT

None ■   b. List all property which has been in the hands of a custodian, receiver, or court-appointed official within **one year** immediately preceding the commencement of this case. (Married debtors filing under chapter 12 or chapter 13 must include information concerning property of either or both spouses whether or not a joint petition is filed, unless the spouses are separated and a joint petition is not filed.)

NAME AND ADDRESS OF CUSTODIAN	NAME AND LOCATION OF COURT CASE TITLE & NUMBER	DATE OF ORDER	DESCRIPTION AND VALUE OF PROPERTY

7. Gifts

None ☐   List all gifts or charitable contributions made within **one year** immediately preceding the commencement of this case except ordinary and usual gifts to family members aggregating less than $200 in value per individual family member and charitable contributions aggregating less than $100 per recipient. (Married debtors filing under chapter 12 or chapter 13 must include gifts or contributions by either or both spouses whether or not a joint petition is filed, unless the spouses are separated and a joint petition is not filed.)

NAME AND ADDRESS OF PERSON OR ORGANIZATION	RELATIONSHIP TO DEBTOR, IF ANY	DATE OF GIFT	DESCRIPTION AND VALUE OF GIFT
Trinity Church **674 Littleton Court** **Falls Church, VA 22040**		**regular weekly contributions over past 12 months**	**$660**

8. Losses

None ■   List all losses from fire, theft, other casualty or gambling within **one year** immediately preceding the commencement of this case **or since the commencement of this case.** (Married debtors filing under chapter 12 or chapter 13 must include losses by either or both spouses whether or not a joint petition is filed, unless the spouses are separated and a joint petition is not filed.)

DESCRIPTION AND VALUE OF PROPERTY	DESCRIPTION OF CIRCUMSTANCES AND, IF LOSS WAS COVERED IN WHOLE OR IN PART BY INSURANCE, GIVE PARTICULARS	DATE OF LOSS

9. Payments related to debt counseling or bankruptcy

None ☐   List all payments made or property transferred by or on behalf of the debtor to any persons, including attorneys, for consultation concerning debt consolidation, relief under the bankruptcy law or preparation of the petition in bankruptcy within **one year** immediately preceding the commencement of this case.

NAME AND ADDRESS OF PAYEE	DATE OF PAYMENT, NAME OF PAYOR IF OTHER THAN DEBTOR	AMOUNT OF MONEY OR DESCRIPTION AND VALUE OF PROPERTY
Sarah Solicitor **9600 Litigation Lane** **Alexandria, VA 22304**	**5/12/05**	**$900**

10. Other transfers

None

List all other property, other than property transferred in the ordinary course of the business or financial affairs of the debtor, transferred either absolutely or as security within **one year** immediately preceding the commencement of this case. (Married debtors filing under chapter 12 or chapter 13 must include transfers by either or both spouses whether or not a joint petition is filed, unless the spouses are separated and a joint petition is not filed.)

NAME AND ADDRESS OF TRANSFEREE, RELATIONSHIP TO DEBTOR	DATE	DESCRIBE PROPERTY TRANSFERRED AND VALUE RECEIVED

11. Closed financial accounts

None
☐
List all financial accounts and instruments held in the name of the debtor or for the benefit of the debtor which were closed, sold, or otherwise transferred within **one year** immediately preceding the commencement of this case. Include checking, savings, or other financial accounts, certificates of deposit, or other instruments; shares and share accounts held in banks, credit unions, pension funds, cooperatives, associations, brokerage houses and other financial institutions. (Married debtors filing under chapter 12 or chapter 13 must include information concerning accounts or instruments held by or for either or both spouses whether or not a joint petition is filed, unless the spouses are separated and a joint petition is not filed.)

NAME AND ADDRESS OF INSTITUTION	TYPE OF ACCOUNT, LAST FOUR DIGITS OF ACCOUNT NUMBER, AND AMOUNT OF FINAL BALANCE	AMOUNT AND DATE OF SALE OR CLOSING
First Virginia Bank **6402 Arlington Blvd.** **Plaza 2 - Room 822** **Falls Church, VA 22042**	**checking account ending in 7352** **final balance $1450**	**4/28/05**

12. Safe deposit boxes

None
☐
List each safe deposit or other box or depository in which the debtor has or had securities, cash, or other valuables within **one year** immediately preceding the commencement of this case. (Married debtors filing under chapter 12 or chapter 13 must include boxes or depositories of either or both spouses whether or not a joint petition is filed, unless the spouses are separated and a joint petition is not filed.)

NAME AND ADDRESS OF BANK OR OTHER DEPOSITORY	NAMES AND ADDRESSES OF THOSE WITH ACCESS TO BOX OR DEPOSITORY	DESCRIPTION OF CONTENTS	DATE OF TRANSFER OR SURRENDER, IF ANY
First Virginia Bank **6402 Arlington Blvd.** **Plaza 2 - Room 822** **Falls Church, VA 22042**	**debtors only**	**documents**	

13. Setoffs

None
■
List all setoffs made by any creditor, including a bank, against a debt or deposit of the debtor within **90 days** preceding the commencement of this case. (Married debtors filing under chapter 12 or chapter 13 must include information concerning either or both spouses whether or not a joint petition is filed, unless the spouses are separated and a joint petition is not filed.)

NAME AND ADDRESS OF CREDITOR	DATE OF SETOFF	AMOUNT OF SETOFF

14. Property held for another person

None
■
List all property owned by another person that the debtor holds or controls.

NAME AND ADDRESS OF OWNER	DESCRIPTION AND VALUE OF PROPERTY	LOCATION OF PROPERTY

15. Prior address of debtor

None
☐

If the debtor has moved within the **two years** immediately preceding the commencement of this case, list all premises which the debtor occupied during that period and vacated prior to the commencement of this case. If a joint petition is filed, report also any separate address of either spouse.

ADDRESS	NAME USED	DATES OF OCCUPANCY
7234 Lilac Avenue **Arlington VA 22204**	**Robert and Dora Doe**	**9/02 - 10/04**

16. Spouses and Former Spouses

None
■

If the debtor resides or resided in a community property state, commonwealth, or territory (including Alaska, Arizona, California, Idaho, Louisiana, Nevada, New Mexico, Puerto Rico, Texas, Washington, or Wisconsin) within the **six-year period** immediately preceding the commencement of the case, identify the name of the debtor's spouse and of any former spouse who resides or resided with the debtor in the community property state.

NAME

17. Environmental Information.

For the purpose of this question, the following definitions apply:

"Environmental Law" means any federal, state, or local statute or regulation regulating pollution, contamination, releases of hazardous or toxic substances, wastes or material into the air, land, soil, surface water, groundwater, or other medium, including, but not limited to, statutes or regulations regulating the cleanup of these substances, wastes, or material.

"Site" means any location, facility, or property as defined under any Environmental Law, whether or not presently or formerly owned or operated by the debtor, including, but not limited to, disposal sites.

"Hazardous Material" means anything defined as a hazardous waste, hazardous substance, toxic substance, hazardous material, pollutant, or contaminant or similar term under an Environmental Law

None
■

a. List the name and address of every site for which the debtor has received notice in writing by a governmental unit that it may be liable or potentially liable under or in violation of an Environmental Law. Indicate the governmental unit, the date of the notice, and, if known, the Environmental Law:

SITE NAME AND ADDRESS	NAME AND ADDRESS OF GOVERNMENTAL UNIT	DATE OF NOTICE	ENVIRONMENTAL LAW

None
■

b. List the name and address of every site for which the debtor provided notice to a governmental unit of a release of Hazardous Material. Indicate the governmental unit to which the notice was sent and the date of the notice.

SITE NAME AND ADDRESS	NAME AND ADDRESS OF GOVERNMENTAL UNIT	DATE OF NOTICE	ENVIRONMENTAL LAW

None
■

c. List all judicial or administrative proceedings, including settlements or orders, under any Environmental Law with respect to which the debtor is or was a party. Indicate the name and address of the governmental unit that is or was a party to the proceeding, and the docket number.

NAME AND ADDRESS OF GOVERNMENTAL UNIT	DOCKET NUMBER	STATUS OR DISPOSITION

18 . Nature, location and name of business

None ■   a. If the debtor is an individual, list the names, addresses, taxpayer identification numbers, nature of the businesses, and beginning and ending dates of all businesses in which the debtor was an officer, director, partner, or managing executive of a corporation, partnership, sole proprietorship, or was a self-employed professional within the **six years** immediately preceding the commencement of this case, or in which the debtor owned 5 percent or more of the voting or equity securities within the **six years** immediately preceding the commencement of this case.

If the debtor is a partnership, list the names, addresses, taxpayer identification numbers, nature of the businesses, and beginning and ending dates of all businesses in which the debtor was a partner or owned 5 percent or more of the voting or equity securities, within the **six years** immediately preceding the commencement of this case.

If the debtor is a corporation, list the names, addresses, taxpayer identification numbers, nature of the businesses, and beginning and ending dates of all businesses in which the debtor was a partner or owned 5 percent or more of the voting or equity securities within the **six years** immediately preceding the commencement of this case.

NAME	TAXPAYER I.D. NO. (EIN)	ADDRESS	NATURE OF BUSINESS	BEGINNING AND ENDING DATES

None ■   b. Identify any business listed in response to subdivision a., above, that is "single asset real estate" as defined in 11 U.S.C. § 101.

NAME	ADDRESS

The following questions are to be completed by every debtor that is a corporation or partnership and by any individual debtor who is or has been, within the **six years** immediately preceding the commencement of this case, any of the following: an officer, director, managing executive, or owner of more than 5 percent of the voting or equity securities of a corporation; a partner, other than a limited partner, of a partnership; a sole proprietor or otherwise self-employed.

*(An individual or joint debtor should complete this portion of the statement **only** if the debtor is or has been in business, as defined above, within the six years immediately preceding the commencement of this case. A debtor who has not been in business within those six years should go directly to the signature page.)*

19. Books, records and financial statements

None ■   a. List all bookkeepers and accountants who within the **two years** immediately preceding the filing of this bankruptcy case kept or supervised the keeping of books of account and records of the debtor.

NAME AND ADDRESS	DATES SERVICES RENDERED

None ■   b. List all firms or individuals who within the **two years** immediately preceding the filing of this bankruptcy case have audited the books of account and records, or prepared a financial statement of the debtor.

NAME	ADDRESS	DATES SERVICES RENDERED

None ■   c. List all firms or individuals who at the time of the commencement of this case were in possession of the books of account and records of the debtor. If any of the books of account and records are not available, explain.

NAME	ADDRESS

None ■   d. List all financial institutions, creditors and other parties, including mercantile and trade agencies, to whom a financial statement was issued within the **two years** immediately preceding the commencement of this case by the debtor.

NAME AND ADDRESS	DATE ISSUED

20. Inventories

None ■   a. List the dates of the last two inventories taken of your property, the name of the person who supervised the taking of each inventory, and the dollar amount and basis of each inventory.

DATE OF INVENTORY	INVENTORY SUPERVISOR	DOLLAR AMOUNT OF INVENTORY (Specify cost, market or other basis)

None ■ b. List the name and address of the person having possession of the records of each of the two inventories reported in a., above.

DATE OF INVENTORY

NAME AND ADDRESSES OF CUSTODIAN OF INVENTORY
RECORDS

21 . Current Partners, Officers, Directors and Shareholders

None ■ a. If the debtor is a partnership, list the nature and percentage of partnership interest of each member of the partnership.

NAME AND ADDRESS   NATURE OF INTEREST   PERCENTAGE OF INTEREST

None ■ b. If the debtor is a corporation, list all officers and directors of the corporation, and each stockholder who directly or indirectly owns, controls, or holds 5 percent or more of the voting or equity securities of the corporation.

NAME AND ADDRESS   TITLE

NATURE AND PERCENTAGE
OF STOCK OWNERSHIP

22 . Former partners, officers, directors and shareholders

None ■ a. If the debtor is a partnership, list each member who withdrew from the partnership within **one year** immediately preceding the commencement of this case.

NAME   ADDRESS   DATE OF WITHDRAWAL

None ■ b. If the debtor is a corporation, list all officers, or directors whose relationship with the corporation terminated within **one year** immediately preceding the commencement of this case.

NAME AND ADDRESS   TITLE   DATE OF TERMINATION

23 . Withdrawals from a partnership or distributions by a corporation

None ■ If the debtor is a partnership or corporation, list all withdrawals or distributions credited or given to an insider, including compensation in any form, bonuses, loans, stock redemptions, options exercised and any other perquisite during **one year** immediately preceding the commencement of this case.

NAME & ADDRESS
OF RECIPIENT,   DATE AND PURPOSE
RELATIONSHIP TO DEBTOR   OF WITHDRAWAL

AMOUNT OF MONEY
OR DESCRIPTION AND
VALUE OF PROPERTY

24. Tax Consolidation Group.

None ■ If the debtor is a corporation, list the name and federal taxpayer identification number of the parent corporation of any consolidated group for tax purposes of which the debtor has been a member at any time within the **six-year period** immediately preceding the commencement of the case.

NAME OF PARENT CORPORATION   TAXPAYER IDENTIFICATION NUMBER

25. Pension Funds.

None ■ If the debtor is not an individual, list the name and federal taxpayer identification number of any pension fund to which the debtor, as an employer, has been responsible for contributing at any time within the **six-year period** immediately preceding the commencement of the case.

NAME OF PENSION FUND   TAXPAYER IDENTIFICATION NUMBER

DECLARATION UNDER PENALTY OF PERJURY BY INDIVIDUAL DEBTOR

I declare under penalty of perjury that I have read the answers contained in the foregoing statement of financial affairs and any attachments thereto and that they are true and correct.

Date **December 10, 2004**   Signature _____
                                              Robert John Doe
                                              Debtor

Date **December 10, 2004**   Signature _____
                                              Dora Jean Doe
                                              Joint Debtor

Penalty for making a false statement: Fine of up to $500,000 or imprisonment for up to 5 years, or both. 18 U.S.C. §§ 152 and 3571

Official Form 8
(12/03)

United States Bankruptcy Court
Eastern District of Virginia

In re   **Robert John Doe**
Dora Jean Doe   Case No. _____

                                     Debtor(s)   Chapter   **7** _____

CHAPTER 7 INDIVIDUAL DEBTOR'S STATEMENT OF INTENTION

1. I have filed a schedule of assets and liabilities which includes consumer debts secured by property of the estate.

2. I intend to do the following with respect to the property of the estate which secures those consumer debts:

     a. Property to Be Surrendered.

     Description of Property   **Creditor's name**
     -NONE-

     b. Property to Be Retained   *[Check any applicable statement.]*

		Property is claimed as exempt	Property will be redeemed pursuant to 11 U.S.C. § 722	Debt will be reaffirmed pursuant to 11 U.S.C. § 524(c)
Description of Property	Creditor's Name			
1. **2003 Honda Civic - good condition, 37,800 miles - in debtors' possession**	**Honda Finance Corp.**			**X**

Official Form 8
(12/03)

In re   **Robert John Doe**
      Dora Jean Doe _____   Case No. _____
                                       Debtor(s)

CHAPTER 7 INDIVIDUAL DEBTOR'S STATEMENT OF INTENTION

Date **December 10, 2004** _____   Signature _____
                                                  Robert John Doe
                                                  Debtor

Date **December 10, 2004** _____   Signature _____
                                                  Dora Jean Doe
                                                  Joint Debtor

United States Bankruptcy Court
Eastern District of Virginia

In re   **Robert John Doe**
          Dora Jean Doe   Case No. _____
                                      Debtor(s)   Chapter   **7** _____

DISCLOSURE OF COMPENSATION OF ATTORNEY FOR DEBTOR(S)

1. Pursuant to 11 U.S.C. § 329(a) and Bankruptcy Rule 2016(b), I certify that I am the attorney for the above-named debtor(s) and that compensation paid to me, for services rendered or to be rendered on behalf of the debtor(s) in contemplation of or in connection with the bankruptcy case is as follows:

    For legal services, I have agreed to accept .... $ _____**900.00**

    Prior to the filing of this statement I have received $ _____**900.00**

    Balance Due .... $ _____**0.00**

2. $___**274.00**___ of the filing fee has been paid.

3. The source of the compensation paid to me was:

    ■ Debtor   ☐ Other *(specify)*

4. The source of compensation to be paid to me is:

    ■ Debtor   ☐ Other *(specify)*

5. ■ I have not agreed to share the above-disclosed compensation with any other person unless they are members and associates of my law firm.

    ☐ I have agreed to share the above-disclosed compensation with a person or persons who are not members or associates of my law firm. A copy of the agreement, together with a list of the names of the people sharing in the compensation, is attached.

6. In return for the above-disclosed fee, I have agreed to render legal service for all aspects of the bankruptcy case, including:
    a. Analysis of the debtor's financial situation, and rendering advice to the debtor in determining whether to file a petition in bankruptcy;
    b. Preparation and filing of any petition, schedules, statement of affairs and plan which may be required;
    c. Representation of the debtor at the meeting of creditors and confirmation hearing, and any adjourned hearings thereof;
    d. Other provisions as needed:
        Negotiations with secured creditors to reduce to market value; exemption planning; preparation and filing of reaffirmation agreements and applications as needed; preparation and filing of motions pursuant to 11 USC 522(f)(2)(A) for avoidance of liens on household goods.

7. By agreement with the debtor(s), the above-disclosed fee does not include the following services:
        Representation of the debtors in any dischargeability actions, judicial lien avoidances, relief from stay actions or any other adversary proceeding.

CERTIFICATION

I certify that the foregoing is a complete statement of any agreement or arrangement for payment to me for representation of the debtor(s) in this bankruptcy proceeding.

December 10, 2004
Date

Sarah Solicitor
Signature of Attorney

Sarah Solicitor
Name of Law Firm
9600 Litigation Lane
Alexandria, VA 22304

For use in Chapter 13 Cases where Fees Requested <u>Not in Excess of $1,500</u>
(For all Cases Filed on or after 1/1/2003)
NOTICE TO DEBTOR(S) AND STANDING TRUSTEE
PURSUANT TO LBR 2016-1(C)(5)

Notice is hereby given that pursuant to Local Bankruptcy Rule 2016-1(C)(5)(a), you have ten (10) business days from the meeting of creditors in this case in which to file an objection with the court to the fees requested in this disclosure of compensation opposing said fees in their entirety, or in a specific amount.

PROOF OF SERVICE

The undersigned hereby certifies that on this date the foregoing Notice was served upon the debtor(s), the standing Chapter 13 Trustee, and U. S. Trustee pursuant to Local Bankruptcy Rules 2016-1(C)(5)(a) and 2002-1(D)(1)(f), by first-class mail or electronically.

Date

Signature of Attorney

United States Bankruptcy Court
Eastern District of Virginia

n re **Robert John Doe,**
Dora Jean Doe
Debtors

Case No. ______________

Chapter 7

DECLARATION OF DIVISIONAL VENUE

The debtor's domicile, residence, principal place of business or principal assets were located for the greater part of the 180 days preceding the filing of the bankruptcy petition in the indicated city or county [check one box only]:

Alexandria Division

Cities:

- ☐ Alexandria-510
- ☐ Fairfax-600
- ☐ Falls Church-610
- ☐ Manassas-683
- ☐ Manassas Park-685

Counties:

- ☐ Arlington-013
- ■ Fairfax-059
- ☐ Fauquier-061
- ☐ Loudoun-107
- ☐ Prince William-153
- ☐ Stafford-179

Richmond Division

Cities:

- ☐ Richmond (city)-760
- ☐ Colonial Heights-570
- ☐ Emporia-595
- ☐ Fredericksburg-630
- ☐ Hopewell-670
- ☐ Petersburg-730

Counties:

- ☐ Amelia-007
- ☐ Brunswick-025
- ☐ Caroline-033
- ☐ Charles City-036
- ☐ Chesterfield-041
- ☐ Dinwiddie-053
- ☐ Essex-057
- ☐ Goochland-075
- ☐ Greensville-081
- ☐ Hanover-085
- ☐ Henrico-087
- ☐ King and Queen-097
- ☐ King George-099
- ☐ King William-101
- ☐ Lancaster-103
- ☐ Lunenburg-111
- ☐ Mecklenburg-117
- ☐ Middlesex-119
- ☐ New Kent-127
- ☐ Northumberland-133
- ☐ Nottoway-135
- ☐ Powhatan-145
- ☐ Prince Edward-147
- ☐ Prince George-149
- ☐ Richmond (county)-159
- ☐ Spotsylvania-177
- ☐ Surry-181
- ☐ Sussex-183
- ☐ Westmoreland-193

Norfolk Division

Cities:

- ☐ Norfolk-710
- ☐ Cape Charles-535
- ☐ Chesapeake-550
- ☐ Franklin-620
- ☐ Portsmouth-740
- ☐ Suffolk-800
- ☐ Virginia Beach-810

Counties:

- ☐ Accomack-001
- ☐ Isle of Wight-093
- ☐ Northampton-131
- ☐ Southampton-175

Newport News Division

Cities:

- ☐ Newport News-700
- ☐ Hampton-650
- ☐ Poquoson-735
- ☐ Williamsburg-830

Counties:

- ☐ Gloucester-073
- ☐ James City-095
- ☐ Mathews-115
- ☐ York-199

Date: December 10, 2004

____

Signature of Attorney
Sarah Solicitor

☐ There is a bankruptcy case concerning debtor's affiliate, general partner, or partnership pending in this Division.

Ver. 8/22/00

UNITED STATES BANKRUPTCY COURT
EASTERN DISTRICT OF VIRGINIA
NOTICE TO INDIVIDUAL CONSUMER DEBTOR(S)

The purpose of this notice is to acquaint you with the four chapters of the federal Bankruptcy Code under which you may file a bankruptcy petition. The bankruptcy law is complicated and not easily described. Therefore, you should seek the advice of an attorney to learn of your rights and responsibilities under the law should you decide to file a petition with the court. ***Court employees are prohibited from giving you legal advice.***

Chapter 7: Liquidation ($155 filing fee plus $39 administrative fee and $15 Trustee fee)

1. Chapter 7 is designed for debtors in financial difficulty who do not have the ability to pay their existing debts.

2. In a Chapter 7 case, a trustee secures for the bankruptcy estate all your assets which the trustee may obtain under the applicable provisions of the Bankruptcy Code. You may claim certain of your property exempt under governing law. The trustee may then liquidate the non-exempt property as necessary and use the proceeds to pay your creditors according to priorities of the Bankruptcy Code.

3. The purpose of filing a Chapter 7 case is to obtain a discharge of your existing debts. If, however, you are found to have committed certain kinds of improper conduct described in the Bankruptcy Code, your discharge may be denied by the court, and the purpose for which you filed the bankruptcy petition will be defeated.

4. Even if you receive a discharge, there are some debts that are not discharged under the law. Therefore, you may still be responsible for such debts as certain taxes and student loans, alimony and support payments, criminal restitution, and debts for death or personal injury caused by driving while intoxicated from alcohol or drugs.

5. Under certain circumstances you may keep property that you have purchased subject to valid security interest. Your attorney can explain the options that are available to you.

Chapter 13: Repayment of All or Part of the Debts of an Individual with Regular Income ($155 filing fee plus $39 administrative fee)

1. Chapter 13 is designed for individuals with regular income who are temporarily unable to pay their debts but would like to pay them in installments over a period of time. You are only eligible for Chapter 13 if your debts do not exceed certain dollar amounts set forth in the Bankruptcy Code.

2. Under Chapter 13 you must file a plan with the court to repay your creditors all or part of the money that you owe them, using your future earnings. Usually, the period allowed by the court to repay your debts is three years, but no more than five years. Your plan must be approved by the court before it can take effect.

3. Under Chapter 13, unlike Chapter 7, you may keep all your property, both exempt and non-exempt, as long as you continue to make payments under the plan.

4. After completion of payments under your plan your debts are discharged except alimony and support payments, student loans, certain debts including criminal fines and restitution and debts for death or personal injury caused by driving while intoxicated from alcohol or drugs, and long-term secured obligations.

Chapter 11: Reorganization ($800 filing fee plus $39 administrative fee)

Chapter 11 is designed primarily for the reorganization of a business but is also available to consumer debtors. Its provisions are quite complicated, and any decision by an individual to file a Chapter 11 petition should be reviewed with an attorney.

Chapter 12: Family Farmer ($200 filing fee plus $39 administrative fee)

Chapter 12 is designed to permit family farmers to repay their debts over a period of time from future earnings and is in many ways similar to Chapter 13. The eligibility requirements are restrictive, limiting its use to those whose income arises primarily from a family-owned farm.

CLERK OF COURT

ACKNOWLEDGMENT

I, the debtor, affirm that I have read this notice.

Dated: **December 10, 2004**

_____

Debtor

_____

Joint Debtor (if any)

[ver. 9/03 b201]

Office of the US Trustee
115 S. Union Street
Alexandria, VA 22314

American Express
16 General Warren Blvd.
Malvern, PA 19355

Bally Total Fitness Corp.
PO Box 42006
Baltimore, MD 21284-2006

Capital One
PO Box 26074
Richmond, VA 23260

Columbia House
PO Box 1114
Terre Haute, IN 47811-1114

Dr. George Smith
8742 Doctors Lane
Arlington, VA 22207

Fair Oaks Hospital
PO Box 16010
Falls Church, VA 22040-1610

Honda Finance Corp.
121 Continental Drive
Newark, DE 19713

MBNA
Asset Acceptance Corp.
PO Box 318035
Independence, OH 44131

Mobil Oil/MCFC
PO Box 85061
Tulsa, OK 74121-2001

Sallie Mae Servicing
PO Box 9500
Wilkes-Barre, PA 18773-9500

Sears
PO Box 818017
Cleveland, OH 44181-8017

VA Dept. of Taxation
Legal Unit - Office Svc. Div.
PO Box 6-L
Richmond, VA 23282

FORM 21. STATEMENT OF SOCIAL SECURITY NUMBER

United States Bankruptcy Court
Eastern District of Virginia

In re **Robert John Doe**
Dora Jean Doe
_____
Debtor

Case No. _____

Address **426 Happy Lane**
Fairfax, VA 22034
_____

Chapter **7** _____

Employer's Tax Identification (EIN) No(s). [if any]: _____
Last four digits of Social Security No(s).: **xxx-xx-7803 & xxx-xx-4321**

STATEMENT OF SOCIAL SECURITY NUMBER(S)

1. Name of Debtor (enter Last, First, Middle): **Doe, Robert, John**
(Check the appropriate box and, if applicable, provide the required information.)

> / **X** /Debtor has a Social Security Number and it is: **123-45-7803**
> _(If more than one, state all.)_

> / /Debtor does not have a Social Security Number.

2. Name of Joint Debtor (enter Last, First, Middle): **Doe, Dora, Jean**
(Check the appropriate box and, if applicable, provide the required information.)

> / **X** /Joint Debtor has a Social Security Number and it is: **987-65-4321**
> _(If more than one, state all.)_

> / /Joint Debtor does not have a Social Security Number.

I declare under penalty of perjury that the foregoing is true and correct.

X _____ **December 10, 2004**
Robert John Doe   Date
Signature of Debtor

X _____ **December 10, 2004**
Dora Jean Doe   Date
Signature of Joint Debtor

*Joint debtors must provide information for both spouses.
Penalty for making a false statement: Fine of up to $250,000 or up to 5 years imprisonment or both. 18 U.S.C. §§ 152 and 3571.

APPENDIX VI

SAMPLE LETTERS

Letter to Credit-Reporting Agency to Correct Mistakes on a Credit Report

July 8, 200_

Equifax Credit Information Services
PO Box 740256
Atlanta, GA 30374

Re: Report No. 110107356

Dear Sir or Madam:

I write to correct some mistaken information contained in my credit report:

1. Under personal information:
   a. correct my birth date to _____
   b. remove incorrect previous address, listed in your report as _____. I never lived at that address.
   c. correct current employer information, to Wonderful Widgets, Inc.

2. Account #___-_____—This is a duplicate account. Please remove it.

3. Credit Card #_____-_____-_____-_____—This is not my account.

4. Circuit City—This matter was included in my recent bankruptcy filing, and should not be listed in my report. I have enclosed copies of the relevant paperwork.

Please send me a copy of the corrected report. Thank you for your assistance in this matter.

Very truly yours,

Clara Consumer

Second Letter to Credit-Reporting Agency to Correct Mistakes on a Credit Report

August ___, 200_

Equifax Credit Information Services
PO Box 740256
Atlanta, GA 30374

   Re: Report No. 110107356

Dear Sir or Madam:

I am in receipt of my corrected credit report, dated August ___, 200_. Thank you for making most of the corrections I requested.

However, you continue to report the Circuit City account, which was included in my bankruptcy filing last year. Please delete that information, and send me a copy of the corrected report.

Enclosed please find another copy of the 341 notice, the Discharge Order, and Schedules D through F, which list all those creditors covered by the bankruptcy filing.

Thank you for your assistance in this matter.

Very truly yours,

Clara Consumer

Letter to Creditor That Keeps Reporting Debt Covered by Bankruptcy Filing

July 8, 200_

Creditor PDQ
PO Box _____
Louisville, KY 40290

Re: Acct. No. 2903008088

Dear Sir or Madam:

It has come to my attention that you continue to report to credit agencies that I owe you $413, although that account was included in the Chapter 7 bankruptcy I filed last year. Enclosed please find the appropriate documentation. [*You should include with this letter a copy of the bankruptcy notice, the discharge order, and the page in the petition where this creditor was listed.*]

Would you kindly correct the misinformation, and send me a copy of your correction?

Thank you for your assistance in this matter.

Very truly yours,

Clara Consumer

Letter to Creditor That Keeps Sending Bills for Debt Covered by Bankruptcy Filing

June 10, 200_

Persistent Creditor
PO Box _____
Harrisburg, PA 17106

    Re: Account No. _____

Dear Sir or Madam:

I filed for bankruptcy on December ___, 200_. The case number is __-_____, and it was discharged on March ____, 200__. Enclosed please find the appropriate documentation. [*You should include with this letter a copy of the petition where this creditor was listed.*]

The United States Bankruptcy Code specifically prohibits creditors from attempting to collect debts after the filing of a bankruptcy. You might want to speak with a bankruptcy attorney to discuss the implications of defying the court.

Please do not contact me again. If I am forced to bring an action in the United States Bankruptcy Court, I will seek punitive and actual damages as well as attorney fees and court costs.

Thank you for your assistance in this matter.

Very truly yours,

Clara Consumer

BIBLIOGRAPHY

Dacyczyn, Amy. *The Complete Tightwad Gazette*. Villard, 1998.

Jones, Roland Gary. *They Went Broke?!: Bankruptcies and Money Disasters of the Rich & Famous*. New York, NY: Gramercy Publishing Company, 2002.

Loonin, Deanne, Odette Williamson, and Gary Klein. *Guide to Surviving Debt*. Boston, MA: National Consumer Law Center, 2002.

Mann, Bruce H. *Republic of Debtors: Bankruptcy in the Age of American Independence*. Cambridge, MA: Harvard University Press, 2003.

McCoy, Jonni. *Frugal Families: Making the Most of Your Hard-Earned Money*. Minneapolis, MN: Bethany House Publishers, 2003.

Nickel, Gudrun Maria. *Debtors' Rights*. Clearwater, FL: Sphinx Publishing, 1998.

Romney, Edward H. *Living Well on Practically Nothing*. Boulder, CO: Palladin Press, 2001.

Skeel, Jr., David A. *Debt's Dominion: A History of Bankruptcy Law in America*. Princeton, NJ: Princeton University Press, 2003.

Yankee Magazine Travel Editors. *Yankee Magazine's Living Well on a Shoestring: 1,501 Ingenious Ways to Spend Less for What You Need and Have More for What You Want*. Dublin, NH: Yankee Books, 2000.

ACKNOWLEDGMENTS

THIS book actually started several years ago when I came up with a six-page handout to give to my clients. I had noticed that many people were so upset about the prospect of filing bankruptcy that they didn't hear most of the spiel in which I explained the process. So I typed up "Nora's Guide to Bankruptcy" to make sure they had access to at least the basics.

I'm grateful to my literary agent, Scott Mendel, who recognized that my little guide could have a larger audience and set out to find one. I appreciate the fine work of my editor at Gotham Books, Erin Bush Moore, whose every suggestion brought improvement. And I must officially thank my unofficial editor, my friend Sharon Ball, who offered excellent advice and helped keep me on task.

I'm most thankful to Tom Raum, my husband and best friend. He's also a fine writer, so I had live-in editing help as well as love and encouragment.

ABOUT THE AUTHOR

Nora Raum has led a double life for many years now. She's an attorney with her own law practice but also works part-time as a newscaster for National Public Radio. Law was a second career for her. She attended college, and then law school at night, while working in radio during the day. For many years, she wrote a column for a local newspaper answering questions about the law.

Nora lives in Alexandria, Virginia, with her husband, Tom Raum, who is a Washington reporter, and their teenage son, Peter. They also have three grown children and, at last count, four grandchildren.

Index

A

abuse of system, 44–45, 114
active duty soldiers, 48
Adams, John, 13
age and bankruptcy, 35
agriculture and Chapter 12, 13
alternatives to bankruptcy, 53–62
   credit-counseling programs, 58
   debt consolidation loans, 57
   fighting the debt, 59–60
   financial management, 54–55
   gambling, 62
   increasing income, 55–56
   liquidation of assets, 56
   negotiating with creditors, 57–58
   waiting, 60
assets. *See also* cars and car loans; house
   assessment of, 21, 139
   and Chapter 7, 45, 97–98
   and Chapter 13, 14, 39, 45
   and creditor's meeting, 29, 35
   documentation of, 79–80, 146–47, 159–63
   hiding of, 88, 89, 117
   and history of bankruptcy, 12–13
   homestead exemptions, 34–35
   liens on, 108
   liquidation of, 14, 56, 88–89
   repossession of, 15
   sample petition, 159–63
   surrendering, 103–5
   value of, 115
   worksheet, 146–47
ATM machines, 8
attorneys, bankruptcy. See also *pro se* bankruptcy defenses
   checklist for meeting with, 74–75
   fees, 25, 73–74, 75, 86
   and fighting debt, 59–60
   full-disclosure with, 84–85, 89
   liability of, 50–51
   and liquidation, 14
   reasons to hire, 40, 65–68
   retainer agreements, 72, 74
   selecting an attorney, 69–75

automatic stays
  in Chapter 7, 35
  in Chapter 13, 114
  effective date, 97
  purpose of, 15–16
automobiles. *See* cars and car loans

B
balance transfers, 6
bank accounts, 24
Bankruptcy Act of 1898, 13
bankruptcy reform (2005 laws),
  47–52
bar associations, 71
Barnum, P. T., 131
Basinger, Kim, 33
Baum, L. Frank, 76
benefits, 23
bill collectors. *See also* creditors
  avoidance of, 10–11
  and bankruptcy documentation,
    78–79
  and credit reports, 11
  and Fair Debt Collection Practices
    Act, 61–62
  notifications of bankruptcy, 18
  pursuit of payment, 15–16
bills. *See also* bill collectors; debt
  assessment of, 18–19
  and expenses, 20
  unopened, 5–6, 18
books on bankruptcy, 66–67
borrowing money. *See* loans
business failures, 1–2

C
cars and car loans
  after bankruptcy, 128–29
  and bankruptcy documentation, 80,
    81
  and Chapter 7, 26
  and Chapter 13, 46
  and means test, 45
  options, 26, 102–6
  paying, 87
cash advances, 7–8, 85
causes of bankruptcy, 1–2, 127
Chapter 7, **33–37**
  and automatic stays, 15
  and car loans, 26
  Chapter 13 compared to, 34, 39–40,
    43–46
  and creditor's meeting, 29
  and debts, 16, 36–37 (*see also*
    dischargeable debts)
  defined, 13–14, 33–34
  eligibility for, 35–36
  filing fees, 25
  fraud accusations, 111
  hearings, 35, 97–98, 100, 101
  and income, 27, 80
  and leases, 106–7
  limitations on, 20
  and objections, 113
  process of, 16, 35
  refiling, 49–50, 127
  value of assets, 115
Chapter 11
  Chapter 13 compared to, 14, 38
  eligibility for, 13, 40
Chapter 12, 13
Chapter 13, **38–42**

adjustments to plans, 109
and automatic stays, 15
Chapter 7 compared to, 34, 39–40, 43–46
conversion to Chapter 7, 114
and creditor's meeting, 29
defined, 13–14, 38–39
eligibility for, 40
failed bankruptcies, 46, 101, 113–14
filing fees, 25
hearings, 16, 41–42, 98, 100, 101
and income, 27, 40, 80, 98
objections to, 114–15
payments on, 41, 46, 101, 113–14
process of, 16, 41–42
refiling, 49–50
voluntary dismissal of, 114
charitable donations, 45, 55
check-cashing cards, 128
check kiting, 9–10
child support
    and Chapter 13, 46
    failure to pay, 14
    income from, 20
    ineligible for discharge, 16, 36, 40
    2005 law on, 49
Circuit City, 107
Clemens, Samuel, 38
clerks, 67
Coleman, Gary, 121
collections agencies. *See* bill collectors
commodity brokers, 40
corporations, 13, 14
cosigners
    after bankruptcy, 129–30
    Chapter 7 compared to Chapter 13, 46
    financial responsibilities of, 28

costs associated with bankruptcy
    attorney fees, 25, 73–74, 75, 86
    filing fees, 25
credit
    credit-counseling programs, 48, 58, 89
    credit insurance, 133
    reestablishing, 126–30
    scams, 131–34
credit cards
    activity on, 130
    after bankruptcy, 25–26
    amount of credit, 6
    amount of debt, 116
    balance transfers, 6
    with banks, 24
    cash advances, 7–8
    and credit score, 122–23
    curbing spending, 54
    and fraud accusations, 111–12
    interest rates, 51, 111
    maxing out, 8
    paying, 7–8, 84–86
    secured and unsecured, 78, 127–28
    small purchases, 7
    warning signs for bankruptcy, 6, 7–8
creditors. *See also* bill collectors
    and bankruptcy, 44
    and bankruptcy reform, 51
    bankruptcy worksheet, 148–51
    banks as, 24
    blocking bankruptcies, 24–25
    creditor's meeting, 29, 35, 67, 97
    disclosure of bankruptcy, 28
    disputing information with, 124, 197
    fighting debt with, 59–60
    landlords as, 27
    lawsuits by, 11, 23, 59–60, 78

creditors *(cont.)*
    negotiating with, 57–58
    notifications of bankruptcy, 18
    objections from, 112–13, 114–15
    preference for, 86–87
    proof of claim, 41
    and right to file bankruptcy, 24–25
    sample letters, 197–98
    secured and unsecured, 15, 77–78,
        102–7
    and security interests, 107–8
    and 2005 law, 50
creditor's meeting. *See also* hearings
    creditors present for, 97
    preparing for, 67
    purpose of, 29, 35
credit reports
    and bankruptcy, 44
    credit-repair companies, 124–25
    credit score, 122–23
    disputing information on, 124–25,
        195–97
    and employment, 23
    fixing, 121–25
    inquiries to, 123, 130
    and judgements, 29
    and lawsuits, 11
    mistakes on, 123, 124–25, 195–97
    obtaining copies of, 121–22
    personal statements on, 124
credit score, 122–23
criminal prosecution
    for bankruptcy fraud, 117
    for being in debt, 14–15
    for failure to pay child or spousal
        support, 14–15
    fines ineligible for discharge, 36

D
debt. *See also* dischargeable debts
    amount of, 5–6, 116, 122
    assessment of, 18–19, 135
    attempts to hide, 10
    and Chapter 13, 40
    consolidation loans, 57
    documentation of, 77–78
    fighting debt, 59–60
    ignorance of amount owed, 5–6
    incorrect amounts reported, 59
    ineligible for discharge, 16, 36, 37, 40,
        46
    joint debt, 28
    payments on, 11, 26
    potential debts, 78
    reaffirmation, 26, 102, 106
    redemption, 26, 103, 106
    secured debt, 40, 77–78, 102–7
    unsecured debt, 40, 77–78, 86
debtors' prisons, 12–13, 14
"debt relief agency" identification, 50–51
depositions, 112
disabilities, people with
    and credit counseling, 48
    credit disability insurance, 133
    and judgement proof cases, 60
dischargeable debts
    and Chapter 13, 40, 46
    court's order for discharge, 16
    creditors' objections to, 25
    debts ineligible for discharge, 16, 36,
        37, 40, 46
    and fraud, 37, 111
    and 2005 law, 49, 50
disclosure of bankruptcy
    by creditors, 28

to employers, 22–23
by newspapers, 24
discrimination, 23
dismissal of cases
    and Chapter 7, 36
    for fraud, 24, 111
    voluntary dismissal of Chapter 13,
        111
Disney, Walt, 83
divorce. *See also* marriage
    as cause of bankruptcy, 1, 10
    joint vs. individual bankruptcy filing,
        28
    and 2005 law, 49
documentation
    after bankruptcy, 127
    amendments to, 95, 98
    case number, 95
    for Chapter 7, 35
    filing date, 87, 93–95
    forms for bankruptcy, 67
    preparing paperwork, 48–49, 76–82
    reading and signing, 93–94, 98
    sample petition, 157–93
    schedules, 35, 95, 98, 158–76
    worksheet, 145–54
drivers licenses, 23
drunken-driving related debts, 36

E

educational expenses, 45
electronic filing, 94
eligibility for bankruptcy
    for Chapter 7, 35–36
    for Chapter 11, 40
    for Chapter 13, 40

embarrassment, 99–100
employment
    and Chapter 13 payments, 41
    effects of bankruptcy on, 23
    and Fair Debt Collection Practices
        Act, 61
    notifications of bankruptcy, 22–23
    overtime or second jobs, 9
    and wage garnishment, 11, 23, 48
Equifax, 122
expenses
    assessment of, 20–21, 81–82, 138–39
    basic expenses, 86
    controlling spending, 54–55
    documentation of, 49, 81–82, 154
    last-minute purchases, 84–85
    needs and wants in, 54
    small purchases, 7
    spending allowances, 45, 81
Experian, 122

F

failed bankruptcies, 46, 101, 113–14
Fair Credit Reporting Act, 122, 124
Fair Debt Collection Practices Act, 15,
    61–62
families, 55
farmers and Chapter 12, 13
Federal Trade Commission (FTC),
    61–62
federal vs. state law, 33–34
fees. *See* costs associated with bankruptcy
FICO scoring system, 122
filing date, 87, 93–95
financial management
    classes, 48

financial management *(cont.)*
  controlling spending, 54–55
  credit-counseling programs, 48, 58, 89
  and re-establishing credit after bankruptcy, 128
Fleiss, Heidi, 53
food purchases, 7
Ford, Henry, 96
foreclosure, 46, 48, 114
forms for bankruptcy. *See* documentation
fraud
  accusations of, 111–12
  and dismissal of cases, 24, 111
  last-minute purchases, 84–85
  and objections to discharge of debt, 15, 25
  and Office of the United States Trustee, 116
  penalties for, 117
  tax fraud, 37

G
gambling, 62, 116–17
garnishment of wages
  and credit counseling, 48
  as result of judgement, 11, 23
government assistance
  in assessment of income, 20
  during bankruptcy, 23
  and judgement proof cases, 60
government employment, 23
Grant, Robert A., 117
Grant, Ulysses S., 110
groceries, 7

H
Hammer, 126
hardship discharges, 36
harrassment, 61–62
hearings, 96–100
  absence from, 24
  answering questions, 97
  attire for, 99
  for Chapter 7, 35, 97–98, 100, 101
  for Chapter 13, 16, 41–42, 98, 100, 101
  creditors present for, 29, 35, 97
  participation in, 29
  preparing for, 67
  purpose of, 29, 35
  "2004" proceedings, 112
Heinz, Henry John, 22
Hershey, Milton S., 12
hiding assets, 88, 89, 117
history of bankruptcy, 12–13
homestead exemptions, 34–35, 141–42
honesty in bankruptcy, 87, 117
house
  and bankruptcy documentation, 80
  and Chapter 13, 39, 45–46
  foreclosure on, 46, 48, 114
  homestead exemptions, 34–35, 141–42
  leases, real estate, 27, 106–7, 129
  options, 106–7
  post-bankruptcy purchases, 127
  selling, 57
  value of, 115

I
identification, 98–99
income. *See also* employment

after bankruptcy, 108–9
assessment of, 19–20, 136
changes in, 27
and Chapter 7, 27, 80
and Chapter 13, 27, 40, 80, 98
documentation of, 48–49, 80, 153
increasing income, 55–56
and means test, 44–45
median incomes by state, 143–44
insurance
borrowing money against, 56
"cash surrender" value, 21, 79–80
credit disability insurance, 133
interest rates
after bankruptcy, 128
increases in, 111
and making minimum payments,
51
Internal Revenue Service
and discharge of taxes, 37
and means test, 45
spending allowances, 45, 81
Internet, 71–72, 94
investments, 79

J

jail. *See* criminal prosecution
judgement-proof cases, 60
judgements. *See also* lawsuits by
creditors
included in bankruptcies, 29
and wage garnishment, 11, 23

K

King, Larry, 65

L

landlords, 27
late payments, 11
laws, bankruptcy, 13, 47–52
lawsuits by creditors
and bankruptcy documentation,
78
and bankruptcy option, 11
and fighting debt, 59–60
and wage garnishment, 11, 23
lawyers. *See* attorneys, bankruptcy
leases, real estate, 27, 106–7, 129
licenses, drivers, 23
liens on property, 108
life insurance, 21
Lincoln, Abraham, 17
liquidation of assets, 14, 56, 88–89. *See
also* Chapter 7
loans
borrowing money against insurance,
56
car loans, 26, 45, 87, 102–3,
128–29
debt consolidation loans, 57
"payday" loans, 6
reaffirmation, 26, 102, 106
redemption, 26, 103, 106
"local rules", 66, 67, 96
lotteries, 62
luxuries, 50, 85

M

marriage. *See also* divorce
and debt, 5–6, 10
and filing for bankruptcy, 28
MBNA, 8–9, 112

MC Hammer, 126
means tests, 44–45
medical bills and bankruptcy, 1, 127
military service, active duty, 48

N
newspapers, 24

O
Office of the United States Trustee, 116
overtime, 9

P
paperwork. *See* documentation
"payday" loans, 6
pensions, 40
perjury, 87
petition. *See also* documentation
    filing date, 87, 93–95
    sample, 157–93
phone calls, avoiding, 10–11
post-dated checks, 9–10
prison and bankruptcy, 117
proof of claim, 41
property. *See* assets
pro se bankruptcy defenses, 65–67
public record of bankruptcy, 24, 77

R
reaffirmation of debts, 26, 102, 106
redemption of debts, 26, 103, 106
refiling for bankruptcy, 49–50, 127

reorganization of debts. *See* Chapter 13
representation. *See* attorneys; *pro se*
    bankruptcy defenses
resources on bankruptcy, 66–67
retirement plans, 56, 79
Reynolds, Burt, 47
Reynolds, Debbie, 93
right to file bankruptcy, 24–25

S
scams, 131–34
schedules. *See also* documentation
    amendments to, 95, 98
    for Chapter 7, 35
    in sample petition, 158–76
second jobs, 9
security interests, 107–8
self employment, 40, 80
self representation. See *pro se* bankruptcy
    defenses
small businesses, 1–2
Social Security number, 77, 99
soldiers, 48
spousal support
    failure to pay, 14
    ineligible for discharge, 36
    and 2005 law, 49
state law vs. federal law, 33–34
statute of limitations, 59
stockbrokers, 40
student loans
    and Chapter 13, 46
    ineligible for discharge, 16, 36, 40
    and 2005 law, 50
surrendering assets, 103–5

T

taxes
  ability to discharge, 16, 37
  and Chapter 13, 46
  tax returns, 48
timing, 83, 87
TransUnion, 122
Trump, Donald, 43
trustee, court appointed
  attorney's relationship with, 70
  for Chapter 13, 38, 41
  at the hearing, 29–30, 35, 96, 97
  and liability of attorneys, 50–51
  role of, 14
Twain, Mark, 38
"2004" proceedings, 112
2005 law (bankruptcy reform), 47–52
types of bankruptcy, 13–14
Tyson, Mike, 69

U

U.S. Congress, 51, 52

V

veterans, 35

W

wage garnishment
  and credit counseling, 48
  as result of judgement, 11, 23
wildcard exemptions, 34, 141–42
Wynette, Tammy, 101